CONSCIOUSNESS
IS WHAT I AM

Other Writings of Joel S. Goldsmith

CONSCIOUSNESS IS WHAT I AM

Joel S. Goldsmith

Edited By
Lorraine Sinkler

I-Level Publications
Publishers

Austell, Georgia

Published by *I*-Level Publications under a reprint arrangement with
HarperCollins Publishers. All rights reserved.
I- Level Publications is an imprint of Acropolis Books, Inc.
Printed in the United States of America.

I-Level Publications
6558 Dunwoody Trail
Austell, Georgia 30001

LIBRARY OF CONGRESS CATALOGING-IN-PUBLICATION DATA

Goldsmith, Joel S. , 1892–1964.
        Consciousness is what I am / Joel S. Goldsmith ; edited by Lorraine
    Sinkler.
                    p.   cm.
        Originally published: New York : Harper & Row, c1976.
        Includes bibliographical references.
        ISBN 1-889051-04-7 (hc : alk. paper)
        1. New Thought.   2. Consciousness.   I. Sinkler, Lorraine.
    II. Title.
    BF639.G5578 1996
    299' .93 - - dc20   96-31394
                                                           CIP

THIS BOOK IS PRINTED ON ACID FREE PAPER THAT MEETS STANDARD Z 39.48 OF
THE AMERICAN NATIONAL STANDARDS INSTITUTE

Except the Lord build the house,
they labour in vain that build it.
                                        —Psalm 127

"Illumination dissolves all material ties and binds
men together with the golden chains of spiritual
understanding; it acknowledges only the leadership
of the Christ; it has no ritual or rule but the divine,
impersonal universal Love; no other worship than
the inner Flame that is ever lit at the shrine of
Spirit. This union is the free state of spiritual brotherhood. The only restraint is the discipline of Soul;
therefore, we know liberty without license; we are
a united universe without physical limits, a divine
service to God without ceremony or creed. The
illumined walk without fear—by Grace."

                        —*The Infinite Way* by Joel S. Goldsmith

TABLE OF CONTENTS

TABLE OF CONTENTS

TABLE OF CONTENTS

~ 1 ~

THE DEDICATED CONSCIOUSNESS

There are two kinds of people on earth: the illumined and the unillumined, or to put it another way, the living and the walking dead. The living are drawing forth life from the Source and at least in a measure have dedicated themselves to some purpose. The walking dead are living an animal form of life, not drawing forth life or inspiration from anything but what can be found in the air or food. No one really lives, however, until he has found something greater than himself, something to which he permits his life to be dedicated.

If this is true, why are there not more persons of dedicated consciousness? Because dedication comes as the grace of God. No one can seek it. He may desire it, but that is as far as he can go. No one can strive or struggle for it because it is not won that way. It comes as Grace, and that Grace comes when something of a spiritual nature is introduced into the consciousness of an individual. He must learn how to open his consciousness to the inflow of the Spirit and make it a

---

The material in this book first appeared in the form of letters sent to students of The Infinite Way throughout the world. The letters were written as an aid to living effectively in this world through a deeper understanding of Scripture and the principles of The Infinite Way. –ED.

matter of praying without ceasing, not just a period in the morning before starting out to work, but one of continuous dedication to a spiritual purpose.

At some time in our experience, it is necessary to make a choice as to whether or not the spiritual goal is worth striving for. If we decide it is worthwhile, we will make some effort toward that consecration. But our effort will lead us to the point where we recognize the futility of our own efforts and realize that unless we have been dedicated by God, all our self-dedication will come to a very quick end. We have to make the decision to practice principles of spiritual living and to remember them consciously. Then, as time goes on, this practice provides the preparation for the entrance of God into our consciousness.

Opening Consciousness to God's Dedication

In our spiritual ignorance, we did not know that from the beginning the spiritual Presence has been standing at the door of consciousness seeking entrance. Through spiritual revelation, however, now we know that our divine Self is knocking at the door of our mind seeking entrance, seeking to consecrate mind and body to Its use instead of to our use or our pleasure, and to take our home and our business and consecrate them to Its purpose.

Let us think of ourselves as instruments through which God's dedication and consecration are made manifest on earth. Each day let us open our consciousness that God may consecrate and dedicate it. Then, to the machinations of carnal mind there will be an invisible sign. "Thus far, and no further." When the carnal mind, the belief in two powers, sees or feels that sign, it cannot get through because God has ordained, consecrated, and dedicated this individual consciousness unto His use. "No weapon that is formed against thee shall prosper,"[1] if and when that "thee" has surrendered himself to God's dedication.

CONTINUOUS DEDICATION

Every day there should be a period in which we close our eyes, turn within, and invite God to come in. Let us think of our mind as a door. Since God, Infinity, is omnipresent, the moment we open the door, this Infinity floods us, and we are under Grace. The grace of God is the wisdom that comes through, the presence and the power; and that Grace gives us our reward, recognition, and fruitage. But we have a part to play:

Lord, I know You are knocking at the door of my consciousness, and I am opening my consciousness. Take over my mind and body. Be my Soul; be my life.[*]

Then we can go for hours rightly guided, directed, benefited, and blessed. But another period of renewal must come:

"I stand at the door, and knock." [2] *God, the Infinite, the Eternal, the Immortal, the Supreme fills all space and is*

---

[*]The italicized portions of this book are spontaneous meditations that came to the author during periods of uplifted consciousness. They are not in any sense intended to be used as affirmations, denials, or formulas. They have been inserted in this book at intervals to serve as examples of the free flowing of the Spirit. As the reader practices the Presence, he, too, in his exalted moments, will receive ever new and fresh inspiration as the outpouring of the Spirit.

Omnipresence Itself. * *As I open my consciousness to receive God, I am permeated with God-consciousness. My mind is dedicated, my body, my business, my home, my talent, my everything is dedicated by God, and God is using it for Its purpose, for which I am an instrument.*

As we take the higher step of letting God dedicate our minds, bodies, and activities to Its purpose, we will understand the meaning of dedication and discover why some persons prosper mightily in their activities, while others who do not understand the nature of dedication and consecration do not. They look upon these as human qualities of their own, and because they believe they are highly dedicated, they look for great results. If the results are not there, it is because they are more dedicated to self and to personal glory than to God.

The mind and the body, separate from spiritual Grace, are the mind and the body of the walking dead, and man does not truly live until the Spirit has entered. Then life has purpose and meaning because it can now express itself through the individual to "the least of these my brethren."[3] It is not enough to be good to our families; there has to be a higher dedication than that. There must be a dedication to others. There will be no true dedication, however, unless we understand that it is not a personal dedication which is merely a promoting of the ego, but a freeing of ourselves for

---

*In the spiritual literature of the world, the varying concepts of God are indicated by the use of such words as *Father, Mother, Soul, Spirit, Principle, Love* and *Life.* Therefore, in this book the author has used the pronouns *He* and *It,* or *Himself* and *Itself,* interchangeably in referring to God.

spiritual dedication that God may bless all who touch our consciousness.

When we come into the spiritual age, which we are now entering, and open our consciousness to the higher Consciousness, or Fourth Dimension, something takes place that changes our whole nature. We no longer have the power to use our mind or body for evil purposes. Something greater takes over, Something greater than our own integrity; Something greater than our education or environment, and we find ourselves governed by a higher Influence. Then we bring to our every activity the dedication and consecration of our consciousness. While some may use their talent, profession, business, or industry for evil or selfish purposes, when a person is spiritually endowed, he cannot use it for anything other than good.

When we are really weary of the dark side of life and when even some of the good side has not given us the satisfaction that it promised, we reach the place where it is no longer a matter of how good or how successful we will be, but where only the fulfillment of our spiritual nature dominates our experience.

BECOMING AWARE OF INFINITE POTENTIALITY

How do we human beings free ourselves of those circumstances and conditions of earth which govern and limit man and over which he seems to have no control? How does a person bring God into his experience? The answer that came to me and that has formed the basis of all Infinite Way work is that nothing can happen to us except through our consciousness. If I am not consciously aware of something, it cannot happen to me. There may be temptation right outside the door, but if I am not aware of it, it does not touch me. There may be opportunities for success trying to rush right at me, but if I do not become aware of them, they can produce nothing for me. Everything that touches my life must touch it through the awareness of my consciousness.

Although there is not a person in the world who does not have a talent–not one–99 percent of us never get out of the rut of very ordinary humanhood, not because we do not have talent, but because we have not been made aware of it, of its purpose, its function, and its utilization.

We can know beyond all doubt that everyone has a talent, and often more than one, because we did not create ourselves–nor did our parents create us. The Master Christ Jesus never spoke more truly than when he said, "Call no man your father upon the earth: for one is your Father, which is in heaven."[4] There is but one Creator, one creative Principle, which is infinite and divine. It could not create anything of an unfruitful, unnecessary, or dead nature. Therefore everyone created in the image and likeness of God is imbued with some talent or gift of God.

Through ignorance we may have embarked on a business career which proved to be unsuitable to us. Someone else may have embarked on a medical career which was not the right outlet for him, or someone else on no career. When, however, we acknowledge the Fourth Dimension, this that the Master called the kingdom of God, we have opened ourselves to Its influence, and then we are ready to receive instruction.

DISCOVERING INFINITY WITHIN

As we close our eyes and turn within, we find ourselves in a blackness, a darkness, but the very place where that darkness is, is our means of access to Infinity. In our acknowledgment of this we are ready for an impartation to come to us. It does not come from without. It comes from within, and it does not come from anyone to us: it comes from the Self of us to us. It comes from the center to the circumference of us, from the depths of our being to the surface of that being. We bring it about by our turning within and realizing:

Consciousness is what I am, and through Consciousness, I have access to the kingdom of God, to Infinity.

Thus we have opened our consciousness that *I,* * the divine Self of us, may enter.

In our humanhood, there are two of us, the man of earth and that man who has his being in Christ. At this moment, it is the man of earth who wishes to "die daily"[5] in order to be reborn of the Spirit and who is now turning within, virtually saying, "God, destroy my humanhood; destroy the limited sense of myself that I am now entertaining; destroy finiteness in me; destroy that combination of good and evil in me and consecrate me to Your Self. Give me that purity which I had with You in the beginning."

Through this surrender, we are opening ourselves to the divine Influence that It may enter our consciousness and govern us. When we have attained the experience

---

*The word *I,* italicized, refers to God.

of meditation in which the Spirit enters, from then on that Spirit permeates mind and body. The purification process is then begun which eventually prevents us from ever thinking of benefitting ourselves at someone else's expense or doing unto others something that we would not have done unto ourselves. It is no longer a virtue or a matter of self-righteousness with us: it is that we have given ourselves, our minds and bodies, to the fourth-dimensional Consciousness, to this divine Self, and It begins to function through and as us.

No experience can go beyond the consciousness of the individual, and when the individual permits his consciousness to be dedicated to the service of God, that is the measure of talent or capacity that flows through. Even if a person were aware of no particular talent, he would soon discover that one was born in him—not really born because it was always there, and it evolves through his receptivity to the spiritual Source.

As we become aware that God, Infinity, is the consciousness of the individual, It takes over and is manifested as harmony in greater and greater degree. There is then less of the human or the finite about us and more of the spiritual or the divine. This divinity does not always take shape in what is considered a spiritual activity, such as becoming a minister, a practitioner, or a spiritual teacher. Not at all. The divinity that takes over consciousness can operate just as effectively in the industrial or financial world or in the artistic or academic world. Spirit is infinite and functions in infinite form and variety. Industry itself is an activity that comes forth from spiritual Consciousness, and one of the functions that industry performs ultimately is the support of art, literature, science, and music.

As we are touched or influenced by Spirit, the mind and body will function in any direction that can prove to be a blessing to the world. It will put some of us in a spiritual ministry, but will take some out of it and put them back in the business, artistic, or financial world where, in one way or another, they can serve the best purpose. Whatever we may accomplish on earth, we accomplish as we let the supreme Power flow through us, serving God's purpose in any capacity given to us on earth.

In the days of our complete immersement in humanhood, we walked, we ate, and we slept, but there was nothing of the joy of life about us, the freedom or the peace of life. Until the Spirit, that *I* within, entered, we were just the walking dead.

OPENING THE DOOR

I stand at the door of your consciousness and knock. Not only am I come that you might have life more abundantly, but I will be with you unto the end of the world.

This *I*, the Soul of us, of which Jesus spoke, stands at the door of our consciousness and knocks. As we learn to close our eyes and through the darkness within realize that we have access to the gifts and riches of God, to the love and life of God, our consciousness is being enriched. As the days go by we witness the fruitage of it in the changed relationships that take place in our life, in the increased amount of our supply, and in the improved condition of our health. This spiritual animating Influence entering consciousness cleanses the mind and the body and maintains and sustains them in the image and likeness of God. But we have to open the door; we have to admit the Spirit consciously.

To the human being, whatever good happens is looked upon mostly as luck, chance, or accident. Even though some of us may be born with ambition or talent, the fact that the talent comes to fruition is often accidental, and not always by design. Many persons of talent never have the success to which their talents entitle them. Many persons deserving recognition never receive it.

To remove success or recognition from the realm of chance or accident, one thing is necessary: to bring ourselves under the law of God that we may be God-governed. That has to be an act of our own consciousness. No one can do it for us. While others may have a different way, the way given to me to teach is the way of meditation. So I have learned and have taught that consciously opening the ear three or four times a day—it need be for only two, three, or four minutes and sometimes only for ten or twenty second intervals—opens the door of our consciousness. This is an invitation to God to enter. Sometimes immediately, sometimes slowly, but always eventually, the Spirit does enter.

If we are meditating solely for some selfish motive or gain, eventually the Spirit may say to us, "You sought *Me** only for the loaves and fishes. Get on about your business. I am weary of you." But if we turn within for the purpose of letting our mind and body be dedicated to holy and good purposes, then the Spirit will come quickly.

---

*The word *Me*, capitalized and italicized, refers to God.

Gradually, as the Spirit enters, It begins to reveal that "He performeth the thing that is appointed for me."[6] "The Lord will perfect that which concerneth me."[7] The secret of those passages is that He does not perform what we would like Him to do; He does not perform what we want done: He performs what He appoints for us, not that our will be done but that His will be done in and through us. When our work is dedicated by God, it is performed for us, in us, and through us, and the fruitage brought right to our doorstep. When we pray, our prayer should be:

I am dedicating myself to the love of God and the love of my neighbor as myself. I am dedicating myself to serving "the least of these my brethren," and the greatest along with the least.

When God dedicates and consecrates us to His service, we will be better in anything we do: a better lawyer, businessman, banker, minister, writer, sculptor, a better anything.

The false concepts we have entertained of prayer, dedication, and consecration have bound us in every way in life. We have to eliminate these concepts and open our consciousness that we may be instructed from within. Then we will not only be instructed in the spiritual principles of life but in the conduct of our business or profession. We will be better at any work than we ever were before because that spiritual Influence is performing it.

There is no possibility of praying successfully until we ask that the fourth-dimensional divine Will be done in us and through us, and that we have the wisdom to perceive that Will and follow It. Then He performs

what is given us to do, what is appointed for us; then He
perfects what concerns us.

~2~

THE FALSE AND RIGHT SENSE OF *I*

The Infinite Way reveals that God is infinite individual being and, therefore, God constitutes our being. Whatever is spiritual, eternal, and immortal in us is God-being. That which is mortal, human, and finite is not an expression of God but an illusion and cannot be raised up to the atmosphere of Christhood. It must "die," but that death is not what normally is thought of as death. It is the death of the false concept of God and man that has been built up throughout the years, which constitutes what may be called the human experience. As we "die daily"[1] to that human experience, we are reborn into the spiritual experience.

Jesus acknowledged his sonship with the Father, and at the same time denied power to his humanhood when he said, "I can of mine own self do nothing."[2] Can we hope to do more than Jesus did and claim more for ourselves than he claimed? When he was called "Good Master,"[3] Jesus even went so far as to deny that. "Why callest thou me good? there is none good but one, that is, God."[3] The truth is that God, the Father, appears individually as God, the son.

If we were to say that we express God, we would be trying to have some power of our own. But this we do

not have. God, being infinite, God alone can express
Itself, and God expresses Itself as individual being. It is
God expressing, not man expressing, and God expressing becomes you and me in our spiritual identity. God
always is the presence and God always is the power.
Never do we have power, never. All power is God-
power as it flows forth from the Godhead, appearing as
our individual capacity. If it were your capacity or
mine, it would be limited, but because all capacity is
God-capacity, it is infinite.

Jesus understood his own nothingness and thus
became the instrument through which the allness of
God could appear. Potentially anyone who can sufficiently understand the nothingness of humanhood can
in that degree show forth God's allness.

THE TROUBLEMAKER

The reason for discords or inharmonies of any nature
is a false sense of *I*. What problem is there that does not
concern the word *I* or that could not have been elimi-
nated if there had not been a little "I"? If the personal
sense of *I* is out of the way, there is no problem. The
only problem that anyone ever has is I, and if there
were no I, I would have no problem. The troublemaker
is the personal sense of *I*.

As long as I think that I must make a living, find a
home, or decide what to do next year, just that long will
I be facing problems of one nature or another. There is
only one error in all the world, and that is entertaining
a false sense of *I*. Give up that false sense of *I* and try to
find any error left. Entertaining a false sense of *I*, we
have an "*I*"–me and "I"–you, and that "I" which has to

be maintained and sustained immediately poses a problem.

The solution to problems, individually and collectively, is to gain the correct sense of *I*. The word *I* means God. It never means any person. It means God appearing as a person. That person is always God-governed, God-maintained, and God-sustained. It is God maintaining Its own identity as a person, just as nature maintains its identity as a rose, an orchid, or a tulip. God maintains and sustains Its identity as you, as me, and as everyone.

Do not be disappointed with yourself if you meet some person and find that you cannot see him that way. That does happen. It happens in our homes and in our communities as well as in national and international life. The way to look at it is to realize that in the outer picture any change has to come from within ourselves. In each of us there is enough humanhood to make it impossible for us in one blow to wipe out the "I" that calls itself Mary, Henry, or Joel. But we can begin. We can begin today to "die daily."

How to "Die Daily"

Quoting statements is of little value. Instead we should ask ourselves: "How do I 'die'? What did Paul mean by 'dying daily'? Is there such a process as 'dying daily'? Is there such a process as being reborn of the Spirit? If there is, let me get busy with it right now. Let me see if I can find out how to 'die.' Let me see if I can find out how to be reborn and stop quoting passages."

There is a way to "die daily." It is to take somewhat the attitude of the eleven disciples, who had met together to select a twelfth to replace Judas who had committed suicide. As they met, their prayer was: "Thou, Lord, which knowest the hearts of all men, shew whether of these two thou hast chosen."[4] Not one of those eleven thought that he was responsible for selecting the right disciple. Not one person used the word "I." Not one of them thought that it was any of his business who was selected. They were all in agreement: "Father, show us whom thou hast chosen."

If I have a decision to make and say to myself, "I must make that decision sometime today," I might turn to God and ask, "God, show me what decision I should make." With that attitude of "I" doing it, I am likely to make the wrong decision or to make no decision at all. The word "I" is there. Instead, since God governs and directs my experience, should I not say, "Father, show me what decision You have made. This is Your life; this is Your world, this is Your universe. What decision would You like to have made manifest? Show me Your decision." Then I could release all sense of responsibility because God not only would show me His decision, but He would carry it out.

That "I" which concerns itself with how this universe should be run or how God's business should be run is a devil. As a matter of fact, that "I" that we are entertaining is not *I* at all: it is a false sense of *I.*

Whether it is in the form of a decision to be made or of some action to be taken, the great release comes with the realization:

Thank You, Father; this burden is not on my shoulders for decision or action. Show me this day what action You have chosen. Show me this day what my labors are to be for the next

hour, or for the next twenty-four hours. To be right it must be
Your action made manifest as me, Your decision made
manifest as my choice. It is the activity of Your being shown
forth through my actions.

There is a miracle-saving grace in this lesson. There
is a miracle of rebirth if we can drop the word "I." I
know that we cannot do it in one grand burst. I have not
been able to do it entirely in all the years since I learned
about it. There is often some trace of "I," Joel, left in the
picture. I would like to see that "I" so completely
extinguished that I would never hear it again. But it
persists. There are little foxes; there are little devils that
make us enjoy the little "I" so much that we cannot give
it up.

It isn't easy for you; it isn't easy for me; it isn't easy
for anyone. We can all think of some of the problems
that face us and see how "I" is involved in every problem, an "I" so limited in power and wisdom that it
cannot solve or heal it. Now let us consider what would
happen to the problem if the only *I* involved were God,
and in our meditation ask ourselves: "Would there be
such a problem if there were not a 'me'? Would there
be such a condition if 'I' were out of the way? Would I
be in such a dilemma if the entire thing were up to
God?"

In that way we will gradually come to see that there
is no problem except what concerns the sense of *I* as a
person. If we take away that personal sense of "I" and
let *I* be God, then what happens to the problem?

As we are pondering this, we listen for that inner
guidance and direction. While we are meditating on the
idea that this is not a decision for us to make and there

is not even any action for us to take, it makes us open our ears and acknowledge that there is a Father who can direct us. It makes us turn for guidance within our own being. We are no longer with that Gentleman up on a cloud, but in the depths of our own being, at-one with the Infinite, tuned in to the *I* that we really are.

If we are trying to help somebody, what does it do to us when we sit quietly and say, "What am I trying to do when the *I* that really does it is the all-knowing *I* ? It knows what to do about this situation, and It has the power to do it." Again we are keeping our mind stayed on God, acknowledging Him as the Source, Activity, Substance, and Law.

The Personal Sense of *I* Is the Destroyer of a Spiritual Ministry

In a group meditation, instead of our thinking about "I," "me," or "mine," "my" problem, or "my" health, what happens when a number of us sit down and forget that little "I," turn to the *I* which is God, and realize that that *I* in the center of us is the governing factor in all our experiences, and the power is upon Its shoulders? It is the law and the substance and the reality. What happens when we drop all these separate "I" 's and find only one *I* in the midst of us, with all of us centered in God and not on our personal problems? With most groups in meditation, each member of the group is thinking of himself and his problems. But all that disappears in this type of meditation in which there is only *One*, one *I*, governing, supporting, maintaining, sustaining, feeding, enlightening, teaching, revealing, unfolding, and disclosing Its own identity, and all these separate "I" 's are absent.

It has been said that if we could be silent on the subject of "I" for even half an hour, if we could drop "I," Joel, completely, or "I," Bill, or "I," Mary, and contemplate the *I* which is God, we would have the kingdom of God on earth.

If we studied the religious and philosophical revelations of the world, we would never find any deeper teaching than this, and it is because of the depth of that teaching that it has not been maintained in human history. Whenever there has been a master to reveal it, there have been a few disciples able to grasp it. Then with that particular teacher and his disciples gone, the teaching has died out because never in the world's history have there been many persons willing to set aside the personal sense of "I."

We have two examples of this in the lives of Gautama the Buddha and Christ Jesus. Buddha discovered this truth and taught it to his disciples, who were fired with the desire to give it to the world. To do that they founded ashramas where people could learn about it. But this defeated its purpose, and the Buddha took himself out of the world because that word "I" kept bobbing up. Somebody always wanted to know who was going to succeed the master. Somebody else wanted to know who was going to be the housekeeper, who was going to be the financier, and whose name was going to be on the estate. The word "I" came in again, and the spiritual import of the whole movement was wrecked.

Jesus experienced the same thing, and his revelation is found in the book of John. He walked up and down the countryside, taught and preached in the synagogues, on the streets, in the homes, and on the hills, all because of an inner yearning to set the world free. He, too, found those who sought to sit on his right hand or the left hand.[5] "I" came in again. It was not a question of what God wanted, only "I," "I," "I." Then came Judas and his jealousy and probably the jealousy of some of the other disciples. "I" popped in, always "I."

The word "I" is what has wrecked a spiritual work at every state and stage because some student will say to himself, "Oh, that's a great truth. That will put me on the platform, and if not, it will put me at the right hand of the master, or at the right hand of the leader." "I," "I" comes in. Instead the student should say, "Oh, since there is no little 'I,' I don't care whether I'm on the platform or down here. As long as I know that God is the only *I*, I am about my Father's business."

REALIZE GOD AS INDIVIDUAL BEING

Miracles happen when "I" does not enter in. When somebody calls on us for help and we can realize that there is no such person, that there is no such "I," the healing has already begun. But when we look upon a person as "I" and think, "How am I going to heal him or improve him or enrich him?" we have destroyed our effectiveness as a practitioner because there is no such "I." The only *I* is God, and It does not need healing, teaching, or enriching.

If somebody says, "I am sick," and our response is, "Well, let us see what we are going to do about making you well," that is the blind leading the blind. The patient believes in a selfhood apart from God, and as long as we, also, have an idea of a selfhood apart from God, we are both going to land in the ditch. The only way we can experience a healing ministry from a high spiritual level is to be convinced that there is no "I" or selfhood apart from God. If there is, there is no God. There cannot be God *and* a mortal being, sick, sinning, and dying.

We not only wipe out the belief of a physical disease and a mental cause but even the person who is experiencing it, and we come to the realization of his true identity. We do not take a human being and make him healthier, wealthier, and wiser: we reveal God as infinite, individual Being. We are interested in seeing the God of his being come into permanent manifestation. The way to do that is to "die daily" to humanhood, to be reborn to our spiritual identity, and to realize when anyone calls for help that in all of God's kingdom there is no such person, no such condition. By maintaining and sustaining that attitude, harmony begins to appear.

When anyone in our family or among our friends involved in any sense of discord comes to our thought, instead of being concerned to see how much we can help him, we sit down with, "Ah, I'm not going to believe there is such a person. God is infinite individuality. God is infinite person. God is the infinite One, and besides God there is no other."

The real way to help is to learn how to "die daily," and the only way to learn that is to begin with a discipline of what I call "Not-I": Not I! No, this person does not concern me. He has nothing to do with me. That real and only *I* is taking care of it.

* * * * *

Climb into That Circle of God

In meditating, we never take a problem into the meditation—never, never. And never do we take a person who has a problem into our meditation. We leave both outside. We take nothing into the meditation but our pondering of God and God's world:

What is God? What is the kingdom of God? What is the government of God? What is the result of God's government? What is the result of the kingdom of God on earth? What is the real meaning of divine love? How can I live the statement, "Love thy neighbor as thyself"? [6]

After I have told a person that I will help him, which I do at once, sometimes he comes back into my thought that afternoon, that night, the next day, or the next week. When that happens, I know the problem probably has not been met, so there is something more for me to do. And what do I do? I merely say to myself, "All right, get out, and let me get back to God." Then I go back to the God that has no problem, no physical body, no finite life, and no age. I stay right there with God, and if the person keeps trying to come in, I keep pushing him out. I won't let him come in: not his face, not his figure, not his name, not his problem. I do not want that false concept of *I* to come in. I tabernacle with the real *I* of the person's being which is God. I commune with It, but not with the person's so-called human identity and woes. I commune with what he really is, God-being. As I do that, harmony begins to appear.

If I were to think of anyone as a human being with human problems, I would probably be just another do-gooder in the world, and after the good was done, it would have to be done again sometime later. But if I keep the person as a human being with a problem out of my thought and hold fast to his spiritual reality, gradually I bring his true identity into manifestation as his life.

That has been the mode and method of my individual practice. That is why there is a chapter on treatment or contemplative healing meditation in every Infinite Way book. While these meditations may vary, the basic principle in every one of them is the same. It begins with the word God and ends with God. At no place does anything but God enter in. Never does a patient come into the meditation.

When a person asks for help, my response is to turn to God: God. God needs help? No, God is eternal life, and God maintains and sustains Its own life. Life does not need any help from me. Life is Spirit, and Spirit is immortal and eternal. It does not decay; It does not age; and It does not change. There is no room in It for aches and pains. God, Spirit, is the substance of all form. Therefore, all that exists in all this universe is God formed, a formation of Spirit, Life Itself, Truth, governed by the eternal law of God, and it can never get outside the realm of God any more than two times two can get outside the realm of mathematics and be other than four.

My meditation remains in that circle of God. If it is a question of inactivity, I realize that since God is the source of all activity, there could be nothing other than perfect activity because no one has any activity of his own. Only God has activity. God is the activity of being.

No person has strength of his own. Scripture says, "The Lord is my strength." [7] And God's strength never fails, so there is no strength to increase and none to decrease.

A person is in danger of dying? How could that be if his life is God? The life of God is not in danger of dying. No, that cannot be.

Poor drivers on the road? How could there be? There is only one mind, and that mind is the instrument of infinite Intelligence, and it is the mind of individual being. According to appearances, there are many minds on the road, and numberless people are paying the penalty for accepting that belief. I hold to the truth that God is the intelligence of individual being and there is only the infinite intelligence of God being made manifest.

Man has no intelligence of his own. He cannot be wise or stupid. He cannot be good or bad. He cannot be sick or well. Only God is infinite intelligence. Only God is good. Only God is immortal life. I will not acknowledge that any person is spiritual, perfect, or good. I will acknowledge only that God is good: God is life, God is love, God is infinite wisdom, God is intelligence, and there is no person except God appearing.

And so I do not credit any person with being good, nor do I condemn him as evil. I will not have any "you," any person. I will just hold to the truth that God is the only "you" of you, and the only thing that can be made manifest through you is God. But it is God manifesting Itself: it is not even you. It is God manifesting Itself as you, so you cannot even take credit for manifesting God, because you are not manifesting God;

God is manifesting Itself as you—no personal glory, no personal demonstration.

Whatever evil we see has no existence. Our acceptance of it as evil is what is causing the trouble. Whatever of good we see is God manifesting Itself, and ascribing that good to a person and saying, "You are healthy," or "I am healthy," or "You are wealthy," or "I am wealthy," is just taking away from God. Only God is healthy and only God is wealthy. We do not express that health; we do not manifest that wealth: God does. There is only God manifest *as* individual being, always God, and the glory is always God's.

~ 3 ~

MIND IS A TRANSPARENCY

One of the steps leading up to living by Grace rather than by taking thought is to keep the mind imbued with truth. In all the writings of The Infinite Way it has been made clear that we never outgrow the letter of truth, that is, the principles. We must always have them as a rock and a foundation.

At first, we hold to the letter of truth intellectually. For example, we instruct the mind, as it were, to hold to God as one Power. Through imbuing the mind with truth, we are remolding our state of consciousness, and one day we will not consciously have to hold to one Power because it will be so much a part of us that we will not even have to deny any other power.

The mind cannot choose to do this: we must choose, and we must hold to the principle of one Power. Every time the suggestion of another power is presented to us, we answer with, "No, I have accepted God as the only Power." As we abide in this principle, we are rebuilding our state of consciousness. We are "dying"[1] to the belief in two powers and are being reborn into the consciousness of one Power.

Let us take another principle basic to The Infinite Way: one Self. God is infinite Selfhood; God is my Self;

27

God is your Self; there is only one Self. The mind of itself cannot accept the principle of the one Self: it must be we who accept it and keep it in our mind. Every time somebody talks about an evil, dangerous, or insane selfhood, we come back with, "But there is only one Selfhood, and I am that Self." We hold to that truth against every appearance thrust upon us of a male or a female self, a poor or a rich self, a sick or a well self, and as we do, we "die" to the belief of many selves and are reborn into the consciousness of one Selfhood.

Instructing the Mind on Supply and Health

The universal belief is that supply is outside in the world and that we must struggle to get it. But the truth is: *I* am supply. "I have meat to eat that ye know not of."[2] If our mind knew this, we would not have to be given instruction about supply; but the mind is ignorant of this truth until instruction is given us. After we receive it, we keep the mind imbued with the truth that *I* am supply, *I* am the Way, *I* am the meat, the wine, and the water.

Tomorrow the temptation may come that we do not have enough, but our answer must be, "Wait a minute; wait a minute! I am not judging by appearances. I am now judging by the truth, and the truth is that I have meat the world knows not of, and I have twelve basketsful left over." As we dwell on that truth, the mind becomes so imbued with it that we are "dying" to the belief of lack and being reborn into the consciousness of omnipresent abundance.

Many people wonder why, after having demonstrated supply, next year they must make another demonstration of supply, and later another one. Why is it not permanent? It is not permanent because they have not attained the consciousness of supply. They have merely had a demonstration of it by some fleeting awareness of their own or by the benefit of someone else's consciousness, but they do not have an attained consciousness of supply.

In the same way, we can go on being sick every year, have a healing, and then get sick again and have another healing. This is not necessary. What we must do is to attain the consciousness of health. To do this we have to "die daily" to the world belief in two powers and be reborn into a new consciousness of one Power, the power of *I AM*. It is not a Power that acts upon us: it is a Power that acts through and as us.

MIND IS AN INSTRUMENT

The truth is that we are divine only when we have emptied ourselves of the universal belief in two powers and of a personal selfhood which we are trying to aggrandize, make rich or famous. When we realize that the Self that we really are is God, it is clear that Self does not need any glamorizing. It does not need any public adulation or fame.

When we seek after fame and let the world chase after us, we sell our birthright for a mess of pottage. The world has a crown in one hand and a cross in the other, and we need not think it will ever be satisfied until we mount that cross. Every champion has discovered that. As soon as he becomes a champion, the fickle crowd begins cheering the other contender. "Vanity of vanities, saith the Preacher, vanity of vanities; all is vanity."[3] It really is.

We have what is beyond price: our true identity as
God-being. More than that we cannot have. We also
have a mind, a beautiful instrument, a beautiful transparency, and it will accept anything we give it. Let us
keep it filled with one Power, so that with every appearance of two powers, we are holding that truth in our
mind and saying, "No, I accept God, Spirit, as the only
Power."

We take the word *law* into our mind. God is law, and
all law is spiritual. But there are legal laws, material
laws, mental laws, and as they hit up against our awareness of one law, we stand fast, "No! I do not accept
them. I accept God alone as law." As we do that, we
will be "dying" to our fears about other laws and will be
reborn into the consciousness of one law.

Mind is nothing more nor less than an instrument,
which in its primal essence is absolutely unconditioned.
Mind has no qualities of good or evil. It is but an
instrument given to us for our use. Do we not say "my
mind," "his mind," "her mind"? The mind is not you or
I. Otherwise we would not think in terms of "my mind,"
"his mind," "her mind." We each have this instrument,
this mind which is the mind of individual being, the
only mind.

We can think good thoughts or evil thoughts, destructive or constructive thoughts. It is our state of consciousness that determines what our mind thinks, and consciousness is what we are. Our mind cannot stop us
from thinking any kind of thoughts we want to think
because we are in charge, and our mind has to let us use
it for whatever purpose we decide to use it. If we want
to use it for good, that is how it will be used; and if we
want to use it for evil, that is how it will be used. When

we know this, we are in control of our mind, and it is not running away with us.

KEEPING THE MIND STAYED ON TRUTH

In the beginning of our spiritual life, usually when we are on the metaphysical path, we are taught to keep the mind stayed on truth, imbued with truth, and as quickly as possible to drop the negative aspects of life. It is not the mind that is power: it is we who are the power. We are the ones imbuing our mind, and our outer life is going to show forth that with which we fill the mind.

The mind itself is like a pane of glass. It is not a power that creates light; it does not even give light: it is just a transparency through which light shines. And so our mind is the transparency which expresses what we give to it.

As we keep the mind filled with these truths, we are letting our old self "die," that self that fears negative powers, that self that has a selfhood apart from God, that self that does not acknowledge its divinity. We let that "die" and let the individual who knows that he is one with the Father be reborn.

THE UNCONDITIONED MIND IS A PURE TRANSPARENCY

A change takes place in our life when we accept the one universal mind as a pure instrument, a reflector of what we hold in consciousness. If we hold a lie in our mind, the result will be two times two is five. It we hold truth in our mind, we will watch harmony brought forth in our experience. "Choose you this day whom ye will

serve."[4] Our mind cannot choose: *we* choose, and then
we hold the truth in our mind and it becomes a transparency for our experience.

That is why, when we are in meditation, the ear is
open as if we expected to hear something audibly, but
that is only symbolic of the inner ear that is attuned to
God. When I am giving a class, I am not thinking nor
am I using thought. I am keeping my mind a clear
transparency to receive God's thoughts. "For my
thoughts are not your thoughts, neither are your ways
my ways."[5] It is not your thought that adds a cubit to
you, nor your thought that makes a white hair black, but
when you are receptive to that which comes from the
depths within you, the earth melts.

When we are in meditation, we work first with
specific statements of truth. These help to settle our
mind into a listening attitude, and then follows the
listening period when our mind is ready to receive
whatever message, impulse, or feeling God has for us.
We are receiving God's thoughts, God's words, God's
truth. Sometimes there will be messages entirely different from any we have ever heard or read.

In a measure everyone who has been led to a truth-
teaching is already prepared to receive truth. And from
where will he receive it? "The kingdom of God is
within."[6] It is only as he learns not to take thought, but
to be still, that he will receive impartations from within,
some of which will be messages, some impulses, some
feelings, but all will bring forth definite fruitage in his
life. One thing is certain: from the time he contacts the
Source of life, It begins to feed, clothe, house, instruct,
guide, maintain, and protect him.

HEALING THROUGH A MIND IMBUED WITH TRUTH

As long as I acknowledge an *I*, my Self, as long as I acknowledge an invisible and incorporeal mind as my instrument, which I keep filled with truth, if there is anything wrong with my brain or my body, it will be corrected. How? I know the truth in and through my mind, and that truth which I know in my mind becomes the very essence and substance of my body, because mind is the substance of the physical sense of body. Mind is not something separate and apart from that body: mind is the essence and substance of it. Therefore, whatever I impart to my mind, the body shows forth.

The most outstanding example, and one that can readily be understood, is that if a person fills his mind with pornography, his body will begin to feel lustful. If he fills his mind with filth, the body will be uncomfortable. It cannot be avoided.

On the other hand, the person who fills his mind with spiritual truth finds the body becoming peaceful, harmonious, and at rest. Rest is not dependent on whether a person sleeps or not. Sleep is not an activity of God; it is the next thing to unconsciousness and is necessary only because of universal belief. Rest is necessary, but we can rest by filling our mind with spiritual truth. As we do, our body comes to rest and is at peace. It may bring on sleep or it may not, but in this work we have proved how little sleep one really needs when the mind is imbued with spiritual truth.

Whatever the nature of that with which we fill the mind is what the body responds to. If a practitioner realizes the truth about God, man, body, law, and substance, and so fills his mind with spiritual truth that he attains an absolute conviction that there is only one Presence and one Power, he is able to bring healing to himself and to those who turn to him for help. As the days and the nights are filled with prayer and knowing the truth without ceasing, a person's life becomes a continuous living of truth and holding it up to every appearance.

When you begin to look on all discord not as a thing or a condition, but as merely an appearance, good healing work begins. If you think you have a disease or a condition to overcome, you will never be a really good healer. You must learn not to treat anything as a condition, but to treat it as an appearance or suggestion, whether it is unemployment, insanity, cancer, or consumption. Then let the appearance hit up against a mind that is imbued with truth, and you will begin to do healing work even before you are reborn, but your rebirth will then come more quickly.

Hold to the truth. Do not do battle with the appearance, but let it hit up against your mind which is imbued with truth, and the appearance will dissolve. If you try to do something to it, you will become enmeshed in it, because you are accepting it as real, whereas it is not real. If it were real, it could not be healed. If God made it, you could not unmake it. Be assured that what God has made, no man can change. It is only because God never made sin, disease, and lack that you can feel completely free within yourself that these are going to disappear out of your life. They will disappear in proportion as you can maintain spiritual principles in your consciousness, hold them in your mind, and let yourself be reborn of Truth.

If we accept the metaphysical principle of keeping the mind stayed on God, if we hold to the positive side of life and let the negative side gradually be weaned away or allowed to atrophy, we will discover that we ourselves govern our life, our mind, and our body. But we do more than this. Eventually the day comes when we are not thinking any thoughts at all: we are receiving thoughts. And that is where the *I* comes in, the *I* that is God.

When Paul said, "I live; yet not I, but Christ liveth in me,"[7] he meant that he was at that moment receiving life, instruction, dominion, and government from the transcendental and invisible Self. The mind is carrying out the instructions, only instead of our giving the mind the instructions, they are now coming through from the *I* which we really are. Then we can say that we are not really doing any thinking. Thoughts are appearing, thoughts are coming to us.

God is not mind, mind is not power, but mind in its unconditioned state is a perfect transparency for God. If we keep our mind imbued with spiritual truth and spiritual harmony, we will soon find that not only is our own mind a blessing, but also the mind of everyone within range of us.

~ 4 ~

CONSCIOUSNESS

The word *consciousness* is one of the most important words in the message of The Infinite Way, but it is as difficult to define as is God. Any name that could be given to God is not God. Even the name God Itself is not God, nor is Soul, Spirit, Principle, or Love. They are merely words revealing certain facets of God.

There is no way through words to attain an understanding of God. When you have come to an end of words, you will discover that there is Something that is not a word, but is your Self, and that is *I. I* is not a word: *I* is my Self.

When Moses attained the revelation of *I AM,* God was revealed to him, and he attained the experience that goes beyond words.

The Master Christ Jesus said, "I am the way, the truth, and the life."[1] He was declaring *I,* and therefore he could ultimately reveal what Moses knew, that "I and my Father are one."[2]

EXPANDING AWARENESS

When you say, "I," or when I say, "I," the next question is: Who am I? What am I? Where am I? What

37

is my function? This is the mystery, the mystery of the ages. So we search, but to our sense it is clear that you, as a person, are not God, and that I, as a person, am not God. What we know of ourselves with the mind certainly would not permit us to believe for a moment that a human being could be God. Yet *I* is God, or else all the revelations of the world are wrong, but as I know myself, I definitely am not God because I know all my own weaknesses; I know all my own faults.

As I go deeper, I discover that that which I have known as myself and which you know as me is not *I* at all. It is some false idea that I am entertaining of my Self, but there are areas of myself that need to be investigated further. All I have known is what was in my mind and in my body.

Through contemplation I began to discover aspects of myself that I never knew before. Eventually this led me to see that I am not a body and that even without a body, I would be intact. But without consciousness I am nothing. Because of consciousness I am conscious: I am conscious of things; I am conscious of a world about me; and I can identify sun, moon, stars, earth, and forms of human life, vegetable life, and animal life. Beyond all that, I am conscious of thoughts, thoughts that do not concern things: thoughts of love, benevolence, charity, fellowship, and brotherly love. These are not concrete physical forms; they are an area in the mental realm beyond the physical, something in the form of ideas and relationships.

At some moment, I become conscious of a feeling within me that is a reaching out and then a feeling of a response which I recognize to be prayer and communion. I and my Father are communing; I am communing with

Something unidentifiable within–peaceful, sometimes joyous, freeing.

Thus I am conscious, not only of what is in the physical realm and the thoughts and ideas of the mental realm, but now I am becoming conscious of a realm that is beyond things and thoughts, beyond what I can see and can think. I have to ascribe to it the word *feeling*, but it is not feeling in the sense of touch but in the sense of awareness.

All that I have described in these few words ultimately led me to the revelation that consciousness is what I am because all there is to me is being conscious of. If I were not consciousness, what would I be? I do not mean if I were unconsciousness what would I be, because if I were unconscious, consciousness would still be functioning. Consciousness would not have been removed: I would just be temporarily not aware of it.

But suppose consciousness were obliterated, then what would I be? A vegetable, and not even a live one. In other words, I could do without feet and hands; I could even do without eyes, and yet be conscious and alive. But I cannot be rid of consciousness and have anything of me left. Consciousness is what constitutes my being. Consciousness is what I am. Take away consciousness, and I am nothing; give me consciousness, and I am all. I am all that I can become conscious of; I am all that I can include in consciousness, and besides that, I am even more because in addition to what I am conscious of, I am consciousness itself.

But if I am conscious only of a physical universe, I am living on the animal level of life, aware of nothing but physicality in one form or another. This was the stage and state of consciousness of our ancestors in the cave-dwelling, prehistoric days, when man lived entirely by force and physical feeling.

The beginning of the mental era can be traced to that time when man began to discover science, mathematics, the building of roads, temples, and pyramids. That was an evidence that the mind was opening, and man was beginning to live as both a mental and physical being. He was a mental being living through the physical body and erecting a physical universe, but with little or no awareness of anything beyond that. As far as he was concerned, mind and matter, intelligence and form were all there was.

The animal man, originally aware only of body and things, later became a mental being aware of mathematics, astronomy, architecture, beauty, and philosophy. In the same way the mental and physical man, who in reality was never a mental or physical man, but was a state of consciousness at those levels, now broke through the limitations of the mind and became conscious of a higher level of life.

When a person who is partly a mental and partly a physical being receives light, illumination, initiation—call it what you will—he is endowed from on High, and breaks through the barriers of the mind, becoming conscious not merely of a physical and mental world but of a spiritual world.

To some extent, the person knows the pains and pleasures of the body, the pains and pleasures of the mind, but to these now are added the greater pleasures: the awareness and consciousness of Spirit. In that higher state of consciousness, he is conscious of his body and mind, but he is also conscious in some measure of the spiritual realm of life, so that he can now commune with the Spirit. The Spirit of God becomes one with his spirit; the life of God becomes one with his life, and in this communion he can be at home in a realm that the human being does not know exists and would deny if he were told about it.

When I know that consciousness is what I am, I know that the reason I am consciousness must be that God is Consciousness, for I am one with the Father. There cannot be an offspring separate and apart from Its basic substance, certainly not in the face of the mystical revelation that all that God is, I am, and all that the Father has is mine.

BEHIND THE BODY AND MIND IS CONSCIOUSNESS

At first, you may accept merely intellectually the truth that not only are you the physical person you can see in the mirror, not only are you this mental person who can read, write, think, plan, and create, but that except for consciousness you would not know yourself as body and mind.

With your body or your mind, you will never know God, but there is an area of your consciousness that can and must eventually come to know the things of God, just as it knows the things of the mental and physical realms.

In the mystical life, you do not disdain the physical realm, nor do you belittle the mental realm. You realize that to be a whole man, in addition to the physical and mental, there must be that infinite, divine Consciousness which gives you your soul integrity and your love for your neighbor. Did you ever stop to think that as a human being a person cannot love his neighbor as

himself? Have you ever stopped to think how impossible that is? A person might be able to love the neighbor
he likes, but he would be very "choosey" about the
neighbor that he is going to love as himself. Do you not
see that only as the Soul of God is your Soul can you
love your neighbor as yourself and not care whether he
is a friendly or an unfriendly neighbor, but love in the
sense that God loves?

Have you ever stopped to think that, as a human
being, it is impossible to pray for your enemies, and if
you do, it is only lip service? Do you not know that
humanly you cannot forgive "seventy times seven"?[3]
Even if you could forgive seventy times seven, it would
never be forgiveness until you forgave through that part
of you which is divine, that part of you which knows
that humanly you have enough faults of your own, and
as you would be forgiven, so you forgive.

Whether individual consciousness is aware at the
physical or mental level, behind both must be the
Consciousness that is aware, and that Consciousness is
God. Now bring that down to the truth that the Consciousness that is God is the consciousness that you are,
and you have oneness. Then you can relax your personal efforts; you can relax from taking thought for your
life. Why should you take thought when the Consciousness that formed you is responsible for maintaining and
sustaining you? You can relax in His Spirit and His
wisdom, because His Spirit and His wisdom are yours.

If you live merely as a physical being, people will
speak of you as being strong or weak, meaning that you
have a strong or a weak body. If you have risen into the
mental realm, they will speak of you as having a greater
or a lesser degree of intelligence.

But if you have ascended to your Father's house and have recognized that God is the consciousness which you are, then some will perceive something in you of a spiritual, impersonal, universal nature. If they do, it will mean that they, too, have begun to ascend above the physical and mental realms, because now they, also, possess the discernment that only the Son of God has: the ability to behold and receive the things of God, the knowledge of God.

A person who has received some measure of spiritual light has ascended above being merely a human being, not entirely, but he has risen at least to the realization of spiritual identity, and this makes "him a little lower than the angels."[4] As a matter of fact, it makes him an angel.

Angels are really spiritually illumined individuals. Moses was an angel, as were Elijah, Elisha, Isaiah, Jesus, and John. Although they lived mentally and physically, the greater part of their life was lived in spiritual illumination. In proportion as we can see that in them, we have attained some measure of spiritual discernment ourselves.

Spiritual Discernment

When you are giving spiritual help to anyone, if you can become unaware of his humanness and even momentarily aware of his spiritual identity, nature, or form, in that degree you have become the child of God, and are able to know and discern the things of God. From then on, it is a matter of developing, until more and more you are living, not in the body and not in the mind, although you continue to use the body and the mind for the purposes for which they were meant. But you are having those moments of ascension above the body and above the mind—scripturally called being "absent from the body, and . . . present with the Lord."[5] They are moments when the physical and mental senses are absent and the things of God and the laws of God are discerned.

Spiritual discernment begins when you stop trying to know God with your mind and are willing to acknowledge that God is. When you say, "God is love;" or "God is life;" or "God is power," you are building an image in your mind, and this is idolatry. But when you can relax in the truth that *God is*, you are not trying to embrace Infinity within the confines of thought. You are accepting whatever God is as *IS*; and then letting that *IS* define Itself to you.

For years, as I have indicated, I, too, had been using words and thinking that I was worshiping God. Ultimately the revelation struck me that there is no word beyond *I. I* is not a word in my mind: *I* is my Self. Since I and the Father are one, and there is only one *I*, God must be my Self. That makes sense. Something is functioning as Joel, and what could It be but God functioning as the son? *I* is God, and *I* is my Self.

To live this, the personal sense of self must stop taking thought, otherwise it is trying to play God, and that is very dangerous. It must stop taking thought as to what the weather, the business, or the plans will be, and let God reveal His will, His plan, His life.

To return to the Father's house, remember that you and the Father are one, and God-consciousness and your individual consciousness constitute that oneness. In proportion as you are listening, you are consciously aware of the presence of God, the power, the reality, the joy, the Spirit, the life, and the wisdom of God. In your body and in your mind, you cannot know the things of God. Recognizing yourself as consciousness, however, and adopting the listening ear, the attitude of consciousness, you become the child of God that is joint-heir to all the heavenly riches. This is because all that the Father-consciousness has your individual consciousness has.

~ 5 ~

EVOLVING STATES OF CONSCIOUSNESS

There is an invisible substance or essence called Consciousness, which can be experienced, but never defined or analyzed. It has a meaning beyond that found in any dictionary, a meaning that we can comprehend only through our spiritual awareness or powers of discernment.

Consciousness is not only eternal and omnipresent but It is our individual consciousness or awareness, the substance, cause, and law of individual being. That Consciousness is so infinite that It fills all space, not merely on earth, beneath the earth, and in heaven, but It is the consciousness of the entire universe, from everlasting to everlasting, without beginning and without end: unconditioned, eternal, immortal Being.

This unconditioned Consciousness functioned in Its fullness in the beginning. We were the expression of that functioning, and our experience was wholly pure, immortal, and eternal. There was no sin in it, no disease, no death, no lack, and no limitation. It was a pure state of spiritual being.

At some time in the history of mankind, man lost his divine heritage, that is, he became unaware of it. It is described in Scripture as the Adamic experience. Adam and Eve, symbolic figures, represent the human race which accepted a belief in two powers, a power of good and a power of evil, and by accepting that belief they were driven out of the Garden of Eden and became separated from their Source, God-consciousness. That is the belief, but nothing really can separate anyone from infinite divine harmony.

As a result of the sense of separation that sprang up, symbolized by Adam and Eve being cast out of the Garden of Eden, we find a mortal concept being entertained in the form of two sons. These two sons were the mortal concepts of the human race—one good and one evil. With that concept, the human race went deep down into degradation, into the lowest form of human life, even cannibalism in some places, with murder a natural accompaniment of this low state of consciousness.

From that time on the human race, as such, had no contact with God. It was that "natural man [who] receiveth not the things of the Spirit of God."[1] The Master summed it up in these words, "If a man abide not in me, he is cast forth as a branch, and is withered."[2] That is the human race. It is not you or I as individuals: it is all of the human race.

The parable of the Prodigal Son is not an account of a man who left his Father's house and returned. It is the story of the human state of consciousness that left its Father's house to wander on earth, setting up a selfhood of its own, and finally coming to the place of creating such marvelous things that it now wonders if they will not turn on him and destroy his life: "See what a world I have made for myself! I have split the atom; I have created the greatest power there is on earth; and now I am afraid that it is going to devour me."

Frankenstein! The human mind creating its own destruction, bringing itself to a feast with the swine, and not only individually, but collectively saying, "Where do we go from here? Now that we have made this great power, we do not control it: we fear it!"

At this very moment, the human mind is eating its banquet with the swine. It is at as low an ebb as it has ever been in the history of the world. It does not know if it can survive until tomorrow. In the back of that mind, it is wishing it were in the Father's house or wondering perhaps if there is a Father's house to return to. Consciously or unconsciously, the world is reaching out for spiritual light in order to be released from the Frankenstein it has created.

There is only one way to be released. If you have made a poison and are afraid of it, if you have made a bomb and are afraid of it, if you have created an ideology and are now afraid of it, the remedy is to realize that the *I* which you are is consciousness, not form; consciousness, not mind. It is to realize that the consciousness which you are is God, and this divine Consciousness, your individual consciousness, governs all form. So you need no longer fear the poison, the bomb, or the ideology, for the Consciousness that is God is the master of all form. "I [Consciousness] have overcome the world."[3]

Until the Spirit of God enters into a person as an activity of consciousness, he cannot know the harmonies of God, the grace or the love of God, but when that old man Adam dies, the person is reborn of the Spirit. He is made a new man in Christ-consciousness. He has opened his consciousness to God, and God has entered in.

From that depraved state in which men hold one
another in slavery, defraud or steal from one another,
and live by the human belief that self-preservation is the
first law of nature, man has had to evolve upward, and
this evolution has taken time.

Mankind has not yet entered a state of civilization,
although this age is called civilized. But it cannot be
civilized while one nation stands ready to drop a bomb
to wipe out millions of people just so that it can be
saved. As long as any nation denies complete freedom
to any race, as long as any nation has a tremendous
abundance and yet does not share it with the other half
of the world that is starving, that can hardly be called
civilization. No, the human race is an evolving consciousness, and as a whole, it has been slowly evolving
since its lowest point of degradation.

THE FIRST DAWNING OF SPIRITUAL LIGHT
IN INDIVIDUAL CONSCIOUSNESS

As consciousness evolved, it began to be purified,
and prehistoric man evolved into a higher type of
humanhood until some time, thousands of years ago,
light began to dawn in consciousness. Some human
beings began to feel something better and greater than
themselves, something that they could not quite attain.

We have all gone through an experience similar to
this in which we have sensed within ourselves a better
self than we appear to be outwardly. We have glimpsed
the truth that there is a part of us which is far more
divine than what we are expressing in our human life.
Some of us, perhaps, still lose our temper, get angry, say
things we regret later, and then realize how foolish that

was: "I didn't mean it; that isn't myself. I don't like to be that way." Others, in periods of lack or limitation, are tempted to lie or steal and afterwards regret it, realizing: "How could I have done a thing like that! It would have been better if I had starved to death, for I know better when I am in my right mind." This is all the imperfect human consciousness, yet vaguely discerning the perfection which is really its true estate.

With the first dawning in consciousness of the light of spiritual wisdom, some men began to perceive that there is a part of man which is divine and better than his human selfhood.

The first record of this Light, appearing as a person, is found in India, in the form of Krishna who is presumably the first man on earth to have broken through to the spiritual realm. His given name may have been Joseph, John, or Paul, or whatever its equivalent in India would be, and so he was probably called John the Krishna, or Paul the Krishna, meaning the Light or the Enlightened One. But as time went on, the human personality was forgotten and he is identified only as the Light and so becomes Krishna, the Light or the Enlightened One.

Krishna was the divine Consciousness which broke through into the mind of man and then was personalized as if It were a man, but It was not a man. It was the light of spiritual Consciousness which permeated the mind of an individual and brought to light the first spiritual or fourth-dimensional awareness.

Buddha, too, is a word meaning light or enlightenment, the same Consciousness as Krishna. Wherever the light appears, it is that original, infinite, divine Consciousness which has touched an individual.

About five hundred years later, this Light again appeared in the Holy Land. Here lived Jesus, a Hebrew rabbi, who became the Christ, the Light of the world, the Savior, or the Son of God. And so in time we have the name Jesus the Christ.

The interesting thing about this is that the word *Christ* is from the same root as the word *Krishna* and has the same meaning: light or enlightenment. Today the Christ is looked upon as a man, but the Christ is not a man. The Christ is the illumined, infinite, divine Consciousness, breaking through the mind of an individual and appearing as man.

Gautama, Jesus, and the first Krishna, of whom we have no accurate history but in whom we can trace the same pattern, were human beings like you and me. They eventually attained spiritual enlightenment, and thereafter each became known as the Enlightened One.

In India there was never any deviation from the truth that anyone can seek enlightenment or Buddhahood and attain some measure of it. All may not attain what Gautama did, for he seems to have been the fully illumined. There would not be many who would attain the complete and full illumination, but it was recognized in India then as now that anyone can become a Buddha or receive some measure of enlightenment.

When the Christian church was organized with its teaching built around a central character, that individual was set up as if he alone were the only one who had ever attained enlightenment, and no one ever again could attain it. So in the Christian church there is one Christ, whom we recognize as Jesus the Christ, the Enlightened One. This belief, accepted with few exceptions, that no one else can ever be enlightened, that no one else can have spiritual light, has hidden spiritual development from the Western world and kept it in spiritual darkness.

Throughout the ages there have been men and women who have attained enlightenment and conscious union with God, what is known as the mystical consciousness. With religious attitudes in the West such as they are, mystics have usually been persecuted or, if allowed to live, compelled to live outside the church.

What we are interested in at this moment is what constitutes enlightenment or spiritual vision. What is it that Gautama, Jesus, and other mystics discovered? What is the secret of enlightenment? The answer is that mystics discovered that there is a part of man's being which is divine; there is a Light within each person; a Presence and a Power.

Every person who has attained spiritual light has revealed that we are the sons of God, but not as human beings. Those of spiritual vision were able to perceive that the same divinity within them is within every one to be uncovered, revealed, lived, and demonstrated. These mystics have also taught how we can attain spiritual wisdom and bring to light our divine sonship. Accepting their word that there is only one creative Principle makes of us brethren, children of the one Father. This evolving consciousness which has led man up from the caveman to his present state is leading him to his divine origin.

FREEDOM AS AN IDEA OF EVOLVING CONSCIOUSNESS

As consciousness evolved, the ignorant, the illiterate, the slaves, and the nonreligious began to perceive a higher state of being than that in which they were living. They became more aware of the nature of freedom, liberty, equality, and justice.

The first people to attain a considerable measure of freedom were the Greeks, who brought some of the ideals of freedom to full flower. Here we have the beginnings of the great philosophies, including metaphysics and mysticism. But much of it was lost; and ever since freedom has been flowing in and out from one place to another, never surviving permanently anywhere.

It was Thomas Jefferson who said that our very freedom has within itself the seeds of its own destruction, meaning that as men become free and life becomes easy, it is a normal human characteristic to begin to enjoy life and not be too watchful, but rather to assume that because they are free and happy today it always will be so. Such an attitude opens a way, as past history has shown, for the opposite idea to enter and eventually to overthrow freedom.

As consciousness evolved, it aroused first, as in the case of the ancient Hebrews, a desire for conditions that they knew nothing about. They could not know what freedom meant, or justice or equality, and yet their vision was leading them toward it. This has always been true in the history of mankind. Ideals have always gone beyond the living of those ideals, and it is true to this day.

I doubt that there is anyone reading this book who has not had glimpses of his spiritual identity, of what he could be if only he could attain what he inwardly feels. We have advanced far enough in consciousness so that we do know that in our true state we are spiritual, eternal, and immortal, but there probably is not one of us who is not kicking "against the pricks"[4]—against illness, economic lack, injustice, or some form of bondage. We know that they have no right to be; we know that there is Something within us that could break these shackles, but it is not possible to know that until consciousness has evolved to a high degree.

As consciousness evolved, some attained a measure of freedom from bondage to the things of this world. No longer is the call of the world so strong. Moreover, there is an attained freedom from sense desires and sense limitations and a willingness to see all mankind made free.

THE DEGREE OF REALIZATION IS THE MEASURE OF ATTAINMENT

There is a part of our being which is already free and which contains the essence and activity and law of our ultimate freedom. With this realization, which has existed for thousands of years, why is not all mankind free? Is it not because we receive the ideals of freedom, liberty, justice, the ideals of spiritual being and of divine identity, but then something takes us away from the direction in which these would lead us, and we begin to resort to outside measures to help us attain what can be attained only from within our own being?

The first temptation is to use human force—mental or physical force—and begin to combat the enemy, whereas the most difficult thing in the world is to close ourselves in tight and realize that we need not resist evil. The battle is not ours but God's.

Regardless of the truth that for centuries conscious-ness has been revealing and disclosing the ideals of spiritual sonship, we still have been trying to demon-strate it by human means. We still try to find our freedom and our health either by physical or mental power. And yet, the divine Consciousness, which reveals to us such grand and glorious ideals as spiritual freedom, wholeness, completeness, and harmony, reveals also that this self-sustained wisdom, glory, freedom, harmony, and health are not to be attained "by might, nor by power," not by physical might or mental power, "but by my spirit, saith the Lord."[5]

It seems that there are cycles, and sometimes free-dom and justice are on top and sometimes they are on the bottom. Always this will be true while we operate from the level of the human being. Evolving conscious-ness reveals that when we attain the divinity of our being there is no longer good or evil. There is only the perfection of God made manifest, and this has no qualities and no quantities. It is infinite, eternal, immor-tal, and spiritual.

Consciousness has now evolved to a point, already demonstrated by a number of mystics, in which it will be possible for us to be led to the realization and demonstration of our divinity. Not only will we no longer be good or bad men and women: we will be children of God, governed by God spiritually and eternally.

In the beginning, the divine Consciousness was your consciousness and mine, and we had no other con-sciousness than that. We were as infinite, as eternal, and immortal as God, for God-consciousness was individual consciousness, and these were one.

Through the limitations of the human mind, there is no way to understand how all of God-consciousness can be mine and still all of God-consciousness can be yours. This can be understood only when God can be realized as Spirit. With God as Spirit, we can understand that God cannot be divided, separated, or cut up into pieces, but that God is always One, infinite, and God is the mind of you and of me. When Paul said, "Let this mind be in you, which was also in Christ Jesus,"[6] he did not say that we were to have a piece of that mind or a little of that mind. He said, "Let this mind be in you."

"And now, O Father, glorify thou me with thine own self with the glory which I had with thee before the world was."[7] God is infinite Consciousness, the divine Consciousness of this universe, the Consciousness of man and of the animal, vegetable, and mineral worlds. Since God is infinite, God could have evolved this world and all that therein is only out of the Consciousness which God is; and, therefore, we individually have existed from the beginning. We were never born; we will never die because God evolved us out of His own consciousness and that which God has joined together can never be put asunder. "I and my Father are one,"[8] is made so, not by me, but by God. God established the relationship that God, the Father, and God, the Son, are one in the beginning, and that oneness endures forever.

~6~

THE LIGHT BREAKING THROUGH

Primal, original Consciousness is pure, infinite, harmonious, and all-good; and this is the consciousness of individual being. When we cut ourselves off or are cut off from that infinite divine Consciousness and come to have a mind and a life of our own, separate from God, we are no longer under the law of God. Life then becomes a matter of chance, a statistic: sometimes good and sometimes evil, but more often evil than good.

The only hope for a restoration to harmony is to return to the Father's house and be united again consciously with God. Fortunately, this does not depend upon us. It is not our human efforts that bring us back to God. It is the grace of God breaking through. I hope that none of us will ever think that we brought ourselves to a spiritual teaching or that we are responsible for remaining on the spiritual path or for any spiritual progress in our life. This would destroy all our chances for real progress.

If we think of the millions of people on earth who from almost any standpoint are as good or better than we are and who are not on the Path, but are surely entitled to be on the spiritual path as much as we are, it must be clear that we have not come this far because we deserve it or because we have chosen God. To believe that we of ourselves have chosen a spiritual pathway would be egotism in its final stage. No, God has chosen us. The finger of God has touched us, not because we have earned it, deserved it, or are better than the rest of mankind, but for reasons which go back long before our present experience on earth, reasons that have to do with evolving consciousness which always comes to fruition in its own time.

"Ye have not chosen me, but I have chosen you, and ordained you. . . . I have chosen you out of the world, therefore the world hateth you."[1] As we evolve from state to state of consciousness, at last we return to where we were in the beginning with all the glory we had with God before the human sense of world was. It is not our human efforts that draw us back to God: it is the primal Substance, Consciousness, drawing us back to Itself.

This process can be likened to a bucket of water into which dirt has been thrown. The dirt cannot remove itself, but eventually it will settle to the bottom and leave the water as pure as it was before the dirt was added. So it is that the Consciousness which we are and which has had thrown into it the dust of the Adamic dream—the crime, the slavery, the belief in two powers—that Consciousness remains pure and is never contaminated.

We began as infinite pure Consciousness and, regardless of any meanness or selfishness today, there is a Force working in us and through us gradually dispelling it. Over the centuries It eventually dissolved the evil or corruption that had been taken on until one day we found ourselves closer to what we were in the beginning.

We do not choose God; we do not choose the spiritual life; we do not choose to be on the spiritual path. A human being is not capable of such a choice; a human being is a creature separate and apart from God. But at some point in his evolution, the Light breaks through and puts him on the Path. We cannot claim credit for this because, as human beings, we would never be other than human beings.

Spiritual consciousness is projecting itself in and through human consciousness, leading us forward step by step. It is inevitable that some few should be a little ahead of the parade. The grace of God touched these few before It caught up with the mass of humanity, which is not yet sufficiently advanced and may have to live another life or even two, three, five, or seven before it is ready to recognize the Grace already established within.

The cry for freedom and liberty is louder now than it has ever been on earth, and it is not unnatural that the forces that would prevent it would also scream a little louder because in the human picture good and evil are always contending one with the other. But since Consciousness is unfolding toward Its fulfillment on earth, those who stand in the way of freedom, liberty, justice, equality, and brotherly love will be crushed. Anyone who fights against the activities and qualities of God is fighting against the evolving or unfolding of Consciousness.

* * * * *

Evidences of an Advancing State of Consciousness

With the coming of the printing press, knowledge began to replace ignorance, light to replace darkness, and the mind became a greater transparency for the divine Consciousness. Grossness and dullness are removed in proportion as knowledge and wisdom enter, and the mind becomes imbued with ideas and ideals about which it had never before heard.

An example of this is that today some men and women who are important and successful in their fields of work are devoting their time to doing away with capital punishment. Offhand one might say, "Why be so solicitous of murderers? What difference does it make what happens to them?" But these concerned individuals are not thinking so much of the murderer or the criminal as of the effect on the men and the women who either as jurors or judges have to sentence their fellowmen to death, or others who have to take an active part in the execution.

When these men and women who participate in that activity have succeeded, they will almost have wiped out wars by that one act alone of revealing to human consciousness the horror of taking life even legally. Is it not a natural step from that to the realization that we ourselves are guilty of legal murder when in war we send our children out to kill and be killed, knowing that they are certainly going out for no noble purpose. The most that can be said is that we are sending out young eighteen, nineteen, and twenty-year lives to be snuffed out so that the forty, fifty, and sixty-year-olds can stay at home, prosper, and be at peace. How great is the hypnotism in the world when parents believe that they are being noble when they send their children out to war!

It is going to take some kind of a shock to awaken mankind to what it has been doing. But with three wars to think about it has been receiving that shock. It has had Nagasaki and Hiroshima, the bombing of Berlin, Leipzig, Dresden, and London to think about, and other more recent events; and it is thinking. The mind of man is thinking because it has had access to knowledge which heretofore has been denied it. The light of spiritual truth is breaking into the consciousness of man through many different avenues and bringing with it a higher sense of life which we now see being made manifest on earth.

The original idea of social security was one of those human manifestations of a divine idea. That it has been abused and used as a political tool is true, but like everything else, we go from one extreme to the other—from not taking care of those who need it to providing care even for those who are abundantly supplied. But those are temporary problems, and the adjustment will come. Social security will again return to its original idea and serve a purpose which will be an outward manifestation of man's loving his neighbor as himself. There have been abuses of many progressive forms of social legislation, but these will be righted under a law of adjustment which inevitably takes place with man's enlightenment.

These outer evidences of a new state of consciousness, even though they may prove as unsatisfactory as the League of Nations or as ineffectual as the United Nations, are the outer manifestations of divine Consciousness breaking through. Ultimately, the ideal which was embodied in the League of Nations and which is finding expression in the United Nations will come through and operate for practical universal good. When it does, we will see that nothing could happen out here in the world until something from the Infinite Invisible broke through to give us higher ideas and ideals.

Let us not be fooled by appearances into believing that any of these efforts toward good or any of these evidences of higher enlightenment and the outer manifestations thereof are either accidental, incidental, or that they are merely creations of man. Behind every one of these is the spiritual consciousness of man breaking through. It is because of this that it is safe to predict that the day is on its way, perhaps nearer than we think, of a universal brotherhood of man, that ideal of peace on earth and goodwill toward men. In all of this, a spiritual activity is made manifest in human activity.

Those few who receive these divine ideas and who give up their personal lives in order to bring through ideas and ideals of universal and spiritual good will ultimately bring forth a new civilization.

This advancing state of consciousness always finds opposition from the majority because it is the nature of the majority of people to be restrictive and behind the times. It is always a minority that leads the majority out of the inequalities of the past. That is why it takes a long time before there is a sufficient realization of the truth that we are our brother's keeper or that we are supposed to love our neighbor as ourselves to the extent that we actually do something about it.

Within the life span of most of us, we have witnessed big corporations providing hospitals and hospitalization plans for employees, as well as retirement and pension funds. None of these existed in my boyhood. They have all come out of a higher consciousness and a greater capacity to feel for the needs of others. As knowledge and spiritual wisdom come into our experience, we begin to understand the meaning of being our brother's keeper.

THE ENEMIES ARE WITHIN OUR OWN HOUSEHOLD

Let us not be disturbed or alarmed when we see the errors that come in the wake of these forward movements, as if there were any doubt of the outcome. There might be a doubt if events were left in the hands of man, but they are not at the mercy of man: it is God breaking through. Although always there will be men to resist change, in the end spiritual consciousness will come through into the fullest of fruition because it is an unfolding activity of the Spirit which is God.

This applies not only on a worldwide scale, but also on an individual scale. Only what is true of the individual can ever be true on a worldwide scale. The fact that we have been students of truth for five, ten, twenty, or thirty years and have not yet found Utopia should not be disturbing us.

As the first light of truth breaks through into our consciousness, it finds enmity within us. A man's enemies are those of his own household, those of his own consciousness, because as the Spirit, or the light of truth, breaks into our consciousness, It must necessarily wipe out of us our human ideas. Many of these constitute what we feel is our good, and we find ourselves in rebellion against the very spiritual life that would break through. If we consciously knew this, there would be no

battle, or it would be brief. However, we do not understand what is taking place; we do not realize that we are
warring against the higher spiritual ideals and instincts
which are coming into our consciousness and breaking
up the "old man."[2]

We have been told that the highest human instinct is
the drive toward self-preservation, but at the same time
that strong human instinct is the fiercest enemy of our
spiritual development. Why? What is it that we are
trying to preserve of our selfhood except what we
believe to be good for ourselves? And what is the height
of spiritual progress? Not only "dying" to the self, but
losing one's human sense of life. Human instinct says,
"Self-preservation"; spiritual unfoldment says, "Lose
your life." The two are always warring one with the
other.

The idea of self-preservation is the enemy of that
spiritual progress which says to us, "Give; share; donate;
sacrifice. If necessary even lose your life for your friend.
There is no higher spiritual demonstration." You and I
are the greatest enemy to our own spiritual progress
because we insist on clinging to the old ideas of yesterday.

This is not said in judgment of anybody, in criticism
or in condemnation. It is said to reveal that within
ourselves which prevents our own spiritual unfoldment
and which is delaying the spiritual unfoldment, peace,
and prosperity of all the world. It is for the purpose of
telling us not to lose patience with ourselves and not to
expect to reach Utopia the day after tomorrow, because
within each one of us the personal sense of self in any
and every form is still to be overcome.

CONSCIOUSNESS EXPRESSING AS LOVE

As we fill ourselves with the mystical and spiritual writings of the world, which we read because the Light which is God has already touched our soul and mind, these inspired writings bring out in us a reaction of "Yes, yes, yes, this is it." We are at one with them. This is our assurance that we have been touched, that the infinite divine Consciousness is breaking through, and with patience It will overcome the enemies within. It will break down that which would like to cling to yesterday's ideas and ideals and the idea that self-preservation is the first law of nature, whereas the sacrifice of personal interest for the universal brotherhood is the first law of spiritual unfoldment.

We can determine the measure in which divine Consciousness is becoming our individual consciousness by the degree in which our interests are less personal and less involved primarily with our family or friends and begin to include the world. It is always brought to the attention of Infinite Way students that they must never confine their giving to The Infinite Way alone but should apportion part of it for community, national, or international activities. As the divine Consciousness makes Itself apparent as our individual consciousness, it must show itself forth in our interest in those things which bring to light freedom, justice, and equality for mankind and for the entire world.

A few thousand people can change the history of the world and transform human consciousness into divine Consciousness. The spiritualization of consciousness will be through the activity of a remnant who know the truth, learn how to apply and live it, and watch it work first on an individual scale and later on a broader scale.

Behind the physical or visible world, God, infinite divine Consciousness, is pushing Itself into expression as individual consciousness and bringing to light the love of God and the love of neighbor. As individual consciousness becomes imbued with the Divine, ultimately someone, some "ten,"[3] may come to the fullness of that divine Consciousness and lift the whole world.

When a person is living an everyday human life and, for one reason or another, is turned to the spiritual life or to a search for God, he is not the one seeking the Light: it is the Light seeking to break through to him. It is not really seeking to break through to him, for the Light is always there, always available, but in one way or another he has become prepared for the influx of that Light.

In the same way, this light of spiritual Being is breaking through human consciousness collectively so that generation after generation man's state of consciousness becomes more and more a transparency through which this Light can come.

~ 7 ~

ATTAINING A MEASURE
OF SPIRITUAL CONSCIOUSNESS

We are on the spiritual path for one purpose only: to build spiritual consciousness. Although many of us find that most of our human ills and discords disappear and greater harmonies are established in all our human relationships, this is not the reason for being on the Path: these are only the added things that come.

We are born into a human state of consciousness, that is, into a consciousness that accepts two powers. We go through lifetimes of inharmony, discord, sin, disease, and ultimately death, and the only way we can successfully overcome the world of error is through the development of spiritual consciousness. Whether we are beginners or whether we have reached the stage or stature of a developed spiritual teacher, we are still in the process of building spiritual consciousness, and except in rare moments of illumination, we never reach the point of having attained it in its fullness.

There are some moments in meditation when we do attain that full and complete realization, but this is the ultimate of our work and comes to few, and to those few very seldom. It is then that the mystical marriage or conscious union with God is attained. Probably in what is called the ascension, it may be possible to attain and maintain the fullness of spiritual consciousness. But certainly during our experience on earth, and that of every known mystic and religious founder, complete at-one-ment with the Source is rarely attained. So it may truthfully be said of all of us, students and teachers alike, that we are continually building spiritual consciousness.

There is in reality only one Consciousness, but we entertain a material sense of that Consciousness. And what is it that constitutes a material sense of consciousness? It is that state of thought that depends on the outer world for its good. It depends on persons for companionship, on bank accounts, on positions, or inheritances for supply. Always it depends on something or somebody out in the world.

Material consciousness lives under the law of infection, contagion, inherited disease, food values, climate, economics, and government. It believes that a change of government may bring about a change in economic conditions, either upward or downward. Always people in the material state of consciousness are under the law, the law of good and evil.

Spiritual Consciousness Is Not Subject to Laws or Conditions of this World

Before it is possible to develop spiritual consciousness, we must understand its nature. Spiritual consciousness is the consciousness that no longer hates or fears error or evil in any form. We can measure our progress by the degree of our realization that God in the midst of us is the only power. When we can look out at the evil conditions of the world, whether in the form of a germ, a bullet, or a bomb, with a "Thank God, I cannot fear you; I cannot hate you: I can only say, 'Father, forgive you,' " we are attaining spiritual consciousness.

This comes by degrees. Spiritual consciousness is unfolding progressively, deepening and becoming enriched, when we can realize that we do not have to fear error, battle it, or fight it. We have learned that God is Spirit, that God's power is spiritual power, and this is the all-power, the only power.

Spiritual consciousness opens a whole new realm of life here on earth. There is no need to wait until a person becomes old or passes on to experience it: spiritual realization can happen to a child. When it does, whether to a child or one well along in years, it represents spiritual maturity which is not subject to the things or thoughts or powers of this world.

Those of spiritual consciousness can walk through the world and not be touched by it. They can walk in the midst of war and not be hurt; they can be in the center of infection, contagion, and epidemics and never be touched; they can go through panics and depressions and not be affected by them. The reason? Spiritual consciousness is not subject to material or mental laws or powers because they are not power.

To the degree we have attained spiritual consciousness, to that degree are we free of the world's discords and inharmonies. In those brief moments when we do attain fully, there is not a trace of mortal sense. Even the body itself appears as light rather than as matter, as incorporeality rather than corporeality.

Spiritual consciousness is not under the law: it is under Grace. It lives and moves and has its being by

Grace. It is untouched by the beliefs of this world. Those who have attained even a measure of it live more by Grace and by every Word that proceeds out of the mouth of God than they live by bread. The fullness of spiritual consciousness was expressed by the Master: "I have overcome the world."[1] "My kingdom is not of this world."[2] "My peace I give unto you: not as the world giveth."[3]

In the Sermon on the Mount, the Master enjoined those to whom he was speaking not to resist evil. He must have been addressing that to disciples, apostles, or advanced students, because even a spiritual teacher could not rightly go out on the street and say to anyone, "Resist not evil,"[4] for the person would immediately respond, "Oh, should I let a burglar rob me?" or, "Should we let some other nation drop bombs on us?"

"Resist not evil" can be said only to those of some measure of spiritual consciousness, to those who have already discerned that evil of any nature could have no power over them since they are consciously governed by God. God is Spirit, His power is spiritual, and besides His power there is no other power. A person anchored in that truth can look at the germs, the bullets, and the bombs, and not resist or fight them, not try to overcome them or do away with them, but realize, "Father, forgive them. They think they have power."

Can we, in the face of the conditions of the world today, say to ourselves, "I need not fear. These things have only temporal power, and what can that do to me, clothed as I am in the armor of God, clothed in spiritual consciousness, abiding in the word of Truth, living and having my being in God? What power can temporal power be?"

Let me bring it a little closer home. Suppose your community is warned of an impending epidemic. If you discuss this with your spiritual teacher, the answer should be, "Fear not; it is only temporal power. Fear not; God is Spirit, and Spirit is the only power, the only substance, the only activity, the only law. Germs have no power; an epidemic has no power."

God is Spirit, and all the power there is must be spiritual. That leaves room for no other powers: no power left for the germs, no power left for the bullets, no power left for the bombs. Why? Because infinite Power is spiritual power.

Perhaps you, yourself, have lived through some epidemic and through metaphysical or spiritual means have proved that the epidemic was not a power. The germs were proved to be nothingness, and either the discord did not come near your dwelling place, or if it touched you, it was quickly met, not by might and not by power, but by knowing the truth that God is Spirit.

This state of consciousness is what many of us have already attained in a measure, but we will never be satisfied until we attain the fullness, the completeness, and the ripeness of spiritual consciousness. Thinking back momentarily to the days before our study and practice of spiritual teachings, however, we can be thankful for the degree of progress already attained.

One mark of spiritual consciousness is the degree in which we have learned the nonpower of all that exists as effect, whether it is "man, whose breath is in his nostrils,"[5] his germ theories, or his stockpile of bombs. The extent to which we no longer fear these attests to the measure of our spiritual consciousness.

Spiritual Consciousness Recognizes
Consciousness As Supply

Another way in which spiritual consciousness can be measured embraces the subject of supply, but supply on a broad scale. The supply of money is, of course, one facet of this, but only one. There are forms of supply much more important to us than money, even though many do not believe this. We will see, as life unfolds, that the subject of supply touches us at every step of our way and every day of our life.

Living in a material state of consciousness, life is concerned with getting, achieving, attaining, all based on the fact that out here is a world of supply. How are we going to draw it to us? All of human life is dedicated to drawing *to* itself from out in the world: drawing *to* itself knowledge, strength, more years of life, more health, money, more opportunity, or more property. All of human life is dedicated to acquiring.

The truth is that we embody within ourselves infinite supply, and no more can be added to us. Any lack in our lives is due to our unawareness of the truth that our consciousness is infinite. Lack has nothing to do with anything out here. We are infinite consciousness, and what we cannot find in our consciousness, we are not going to find out in the world. Consciousness is the source from which we have to begin, and whatever is to evolve comes from that consciousness. "The earth is the Lord's, and the fulness thereof."[6] "Son, thou art ever with me, and all that I have is thine."[7] All that God has is ours; we have all there is: we have infinity.

In a material state of consciousness, we are likely to say, "No, that cannot be true. Many people have more than I have." But that is only true when measured from a materialistic basis which would divide the existing supply.

In Spirit, there is no division. In the spiritual kingdom, there is only one number. That is the number one, and I embody within myself the fullness of that number. All that the Father has is mine, because of my oneness with God.

Material consciousness sees three and one-half billion people in the world, and only so many dollars, so much gold, so much silver, so many trees, so many crops, and they must all be divided. Spiritual consciousness reveals that if we have only a few loaves and fishes, we can feed the multitudes. There is no such thing as division: there is only multiplication, one multiplying itself over and over and over again.

When Elisha approached the poor widow who had only a handful of meal and a few drops of oil, he did not waste time praying to God to give her more. He knew the spiritual law of supply and first asked her to make him a little cake.[8] It was as if he had said to her, "What have you in your house?" because spiritually, that is the secret of supply.

What have you in your consciousness? Do not look out into the world and see what you want and ask for it; do not have an idea in your mind of what you would like and then pray to God for it. Ask yourself, "What have I in my consciousness?" The only supply you are ever going to have is what you begin to pour. The bread that you cast on the water is the bread that is going to come back as your supply. If you touch somebody else's bread that has been placed on that water, your fingers will be burned.

You are entitled only to what you give forth, just as you are entitled to no more out of life than what you put into life. Anyone on the spiritual path who believes that he can take more from life than he is putting into it is not counting the day of reckoning. Those who have the most, of them the most will be demanded.

Begin to evolve spiritually by withdrawing your gaze from the world and the things of the world, your desires, and your wants, and live spiritually, live from the standpoint of what you can give or add to the world, so that if someday a monument is built over your body or your ashes it will not say that he attained so much in the world, but that he gave so much to the world. Let us build that kind of an epitaph.

"What have I in the house now?" In a spiritual universe, we are thinking in terms of spiritual gifts. One of the greatest gifts we have is the gift of prayer. So if we have nothing else in our consciousness but that gift, we can begin to give in the form of prayer: prayer for our enemies, for the world, and for our neighbor.

There is no one in all the world who does not have some trace of love in him, although there are many people who do not give any evidence of love. But everyone has at the center of his being some love: love that can be expressed in service, love that can be expressed in gratitude, cooperation, understanding, and forgiveness. Everyone has some money or clothing, something that can be given or contributed to those who appear not to recognize the infinite nature of the Storehouse upon which they may draw.

* * * * *

DRAWING ON THE SPIRITUAL STOREHOUSE

Knowing the truth of the infinite Storehouse within, we can draw forth from consciousness, not only all that is necessary for our particular unfoldment, but twelve basketsful left over to share. Any demonstration that merely provides for our needs alone is not a spiritual demonstration. The Spirit does not operate that way.

We can decide to take the first dollar out of our week's income and set aside for an impersonal contribution to community activities. We can decide that since this is not from us, but from the infinite Storehouse, we will increase that outgoing dollar because of the incoming increase which must inevitably follow. But spiritually the increase cannot occur until the outgo has taken place. This is the reverse of the materialistic concept which is that if money comes in, we will pay it out. In the spiritual universe we pay it out in order that it may come in.

This applies to every facet of life. There are many requests for help that come from persons who would like companionship. My answer is, "I don't believe you want companionship. I think you are looking for a companion, and I am not in that business so I cannot help you." Wanting a companion is quite different from wanting companionship. Anyone in the world can have companionship because God has planted that quality in every person, and all anyone has to do is to share it.

Companionship is not something that we get from another; companionship is something we give to another. Therefore, to have companionship means first of all to give it, to give it in one form or another. Whether we give it to human beings, to animals, or to the trees in the park or the rosebushes, we must pour out companionship to the world, even if it is nothing but enjoying watching the sun, the moon, and the stars. Then companionship flows back to us, but it will be the companionship that we have cast upon the waters.

How many of us have for many, many years believed that others were holding us in condemnation, unforgiveness, or holding grievances against us, not realizing that we were doing it, and not they? No one can forgive us while we carry unforgiveness within ourselves. The supply of forgiveness that we are eternally praying for, we are holding away from us, until we realize, "I do not really care whether or not you forgive me. That is your demonstration. All I care about is that I forgive you. I freely forgive all those who have offended me; I freely forgive all those who have spitefully used me; I freely forgive all those who have criticized, judged, or condemned me. Freely I do this because I cannot live with myself without this eternal sense of forgiveness. If there are those who do not wish to see me in that light, it is their demonstration, not mine. My demonstration is forgiveness."

The subject of supply plays a major role in our lives. Until we begin to live as if we are one with the Father and as if all that the Father has is ours, and act that out by sharing our resources, sharing forgiveness, cooperation, understanding, patience, whatever it is, spiritual consciousness has not yet touched us.

BECOMING AWARE OF THE INDWELLING PRESENCE

The study of truth is the smallest part of our life's demonstration. Far too many students study too much.

It takes a very small statement of truth to spark our consciousness into action, and then it is that action that brings about the development of our spiritual consciousness. It is not what we read that does it: it is what we *do* with what we read that does it.

The word of God, the truth in our consciousness, is what we live by, and so, we must make it a practice every few minutes, every half hour, or every hour to pause to remember some statement of truth. Some word of God must be entertained in our consciousness throughout our days and nights, and then eventually we are fed more by those very passages of truth than we are fed by the food we eat. This we may call practicing the presence of God.

Pondering the word of God and maintaining it in our consciousness is contemplative meditation. It takes only a few months of this type of living until a new experience comes to us. Then in some moment of need, when we are not thinking truth, a word of truth will come into our consciousness from the Invisible, something that we ourselves did not consciously think.

At this point in our development, when we can open our ears and receive impartations from within, we are living by Grace, taking no thought for our life, knowing that there is an invisible Presence and Power bringing harmony into our experience without conscious effort.

There is a Spirit that dwells in us. It is invisible, and we cannot see It with our eyes. It is incorporeal. We cannot even feel It, but we can experience It; we can know It is there by Its fruitage, because with the realization of its presence, we instantly lose all fear. No longer can we fear life or any of life's experiences, nor can we fear death. Neither life nor death can separate us from the life of God, nor from the will of God. Whatever the will of God is for us on earth or on the next plane, that will of God will be done because He has planted His son in us to see to it that it happens.

If this were true of one individual only and not possible to all of us, there would be no true God. But there is God, and the Master revealed this in his statement: "Call no man your father upon the earth: for one is your Father, which is in heaven."[9] This Father is yours and mine in proportion to our ability to open our consciousness to It, to surrender ourselves to It, to be willing to live, "not by might, nor by power,"[10] to put up our sword, to stop being angry, resentful, hateful, or fearful—not that we can do it humanly, but the grace of God makes it natural for all these to disappear from our consciousness.

Open yourself to the truth that the Spirit of God dwells in you; and above all things, stop this theological nonsense of believing that God deserts you in your moment of sin. Heaven forbid! It is then that you need God most, and do not believe that God could desert His own. Never!

In any moment that you open your consciousness to the realization that there is a son of God, the son of God will appear to you, not necessarily in form, but in consciousness, and you will hear the words of the Master: "Neither do I condemn thee."[11] "Thy sins be forgiven thee."[12] Or you will feel that you are forgiven: you are free. This is an evidence of evolving spiritual consciousness.

Spiritual consciousness is a realization that within you is the substance of all that is to appear in your world, whereas material consciousness is a belief that you acquire, accomplish, and achieve from the outside. Spiritual consciousness is an awareness that all you need flows to you from within your own being.

You come to a place in consciousness where it becomes clear to you that you are not dependent on anything out here, but that you must turn to the Infinite Invisible for your good. At some particular time within yourself, you say, "Yes, my dependence henceforth will be on the Infinite Invisible, on the kingdom of God within me. Less and less will I look outside." Thus your faith, hope, and dependence on the outer world gradually shift to the kingdom within, and the material state of consciousness yields to that spiritual consciousness which is "the glory . . . I had with thee before the world was."[13]

~ 8 ~

INVISIBLE LIFE FULFILLS ITSELF TANGIBLY AND VISIBLY

Everyone has the potentiality of attaining spiritual enlightenment. From the moment we open our first book of truth or have our first contact with an enlightened person, our own enlightenment has begun, and spiritual illumination will come to us in proportion to our seeking it.

When the light dawns in our consciousness, we behold God as infinite and realize that there cannot be God and anything else. Otherwise God would be that much less than infinite. God must exist as the substance of all that is. God constitutes all that is, so we no longer look to God for our health because there is not God *and* health. Scripture says that God is "the health of my countenance."[1] We cannot get health, but we can get God, and when we have God, we have health.

I know of no way in which we, through the practice of The Infinite Way, can demonstrate supply, companionship, or a home. As a matter of fact, I sincerely believe that all such attempts would prove to be a barrier to the demonstration of our harmony. Outside of God, I cannot find abundance, companionship, or home desirable. In fact, I cannot find life itself desirable outside of God. To live in the greatest harmony, health, or abundance without God would seem to me to be living a very barren life. God is infinite being, and since there cannot be anything beyond or anything more than Infinity, there cannot be lasting supply, home, or companionship outside of Infinity. There is only Infinity, and whatever is, is embraced in the infinity of Spirit.

How can we think of Spirit or God as the substance of all that is and then go to God to get some material thing? God is infinite, so what is there to get? There is nothing outside the limits of Spirit. How can we go to Spirit to get something that does not exist? Is not the very idea of going to God for something the barrier to its attainment?

It may be that for some reason we are experiencing a barren period in our personal life. That does not mean that supply is absent and that if we could only reach God, He would make it appear. God is omnipresence, and our recognition of the omnipresence of God will, in due course, show forth the evidence of what we call supply. We think of Omnipresence, however, and then we think in terms of the omnipresence of some form of good. But Omnipresence means the omnipresence of Spirit, the omnipresence of the Source, of the Law, and of Life, not the omnipresence of any form.

It would be a mistake to say that Omnipresence means the ever presence of roses, because roses are not always in evidence. True, they are always here in their spiritual essence, but not in manifested form. The recognition of the omnipresence of Spirit will bring the rose into manifestation in its due season, or the fruit, the money, the transportation, the companionship, or the housing. But Omnipresence must be thought of as the omnipresence of Spirit, Cause, Substance, and Activity. The only taking of thought we should do is to acknowledge the omnipresence of Spirit, and then let that realization manifest itself as what we eat, drink, or with what we are clothed—not in what we call *our* due time, but in *Its* due time.

In our human experience, it seems we sometimes have to wait for these things to appear even though they are omnipresent now in consciousness. It is very much like healing. Actually, all healing is instantaneous: there is no such thing as delayed or gradual healing, but the outward manifestation does not always appear in the same second as the healing. If we were to receive an impartation now that brought forth healing, we might not be aware of the healing until tomorrow or next week.

There may be a claim of lack or limitation in some form. We ask for and receive help. It may be a week, however, before something comes to us as the necessary number of dollar bills or whatever form the fulfillment is to take. But because it took a day, week, or a month to see the completed outer picture does not mean that the healing was not instantaneous. The visible evidence is the effect of the healing, not the healing: the healing is invisible, but the visible evidence is the externalized or manifested effect.

The Infinite Way recognizes the search for and the attainment of God as its only goal, thereby discovering the greatest mystery of all, which is that as God is attained, health, harmony, wholeness, completeness, companionship, home, abundance, and the twelve basketsful left over are also attained. The only right desire is the desire for the realization of Spirit. The only demonstration that is possible in The Infinite Way is the demonstration of God's presence, and once we demonstrate that, good will unfold in infinite form and variety. Seeking the form and variety, however, will act as a barrier to the demonstration.

REPLACE THE CONCEPT OF A GIVING AND A WITHHOLDING GOD WITH A GOD THAT IS

Some years ago, a woman came to my office, complaining that nothing seemed to happen in her life. Here she was with a new teaching, and it was not doing any more for her than her old religion. No matter what she did, no matter what her practitioner did, nothing seemed to turn out right for her. One day in my office I said to her, "Tell me, what do you think about God? I mean, do you have the same God now that you had in your church? Do you pray to God in the same way you prayed before?"

"Oh," she said, "I do not pray the same way, because now I affirm and deny, whereas before I used to ask."

"Yes, I know, but are you affirming and denying to the same God? Is it to a God you are expecting to give you something?"

"Oh, yes! God does not change. It is the same God; there is only one God."

"Well, I am afraid that is where you are stuck. There is only one God, but you have not met Him, and until you give up the concept of God that you have, you are going to get the same reaction from that concept, whether you beg, plead, affirm, or deny, and it will be the same if you give up affirming and denying. The result will be nothing, because you are worshiping a God that does not exist."

We have to change our concept of God until we attain the realization of a God that *is*, and a God that is *ising*, a God that is eternally being God, without any urging, asking, or begging from us or without any affirming or denying, a God that is infinite in being, omnipresent in being, omnipotent in being, omniscient in being.

We must come to a whole new concept of God and make a transition from whatever former concepts we have held. God is not going to be any different a century from now than God was a century ago. God was not any different on the shores of Galilee two thousand years ago than God is today. If we are not manifesting the same degree of God in our experience that we could have manifested two thousand years ago had we been sitting with the Master, it is not because of an absence of God, but because of our erroneous concept of what God is, where God is, and when God is. It all has to do with us!

To what degree have we attained the realization of the omnipresence of God and of letting God, divine Consciousness, live our life? To what degree are we still trying to mold God into our image and likeness? Our concepts must be changed to give way to a recognition of Omnipresence, Omnipresence here where we are; Omniscience, the All-knowing; Omnipotence, the All-power. Then we can relax and be. All there is to do is to *be* and to awaken in the morning in the realization:

I am living here and now, and the Spirit of God that dwells in me goes before me to perfect this day. He performs all that is given me to do; He perfects that which concerns me. My only function is to be *and to bear witness.*

As we stand still and bear witness, our good will unfold from an invisible Source through an invisible Power operating on the visible universe. It is God that brings up the sun; it is God that awakens the buds and brings them into full bloom; it is God that is invisibly working to put fruit on the tree. That same God is invisibly working in us to bring forth God's fruitage as our individual life.

You and I are not all supposed to be merely mothers or fathers, businessmen, ministers, or practitioners. Each one of us is to show forth God's glory in an individual way, and who are we to dictate to God what we would like to be or what we would like to do or where we would like to do it? Have we not watched the seasons change, the coming and the going of day and night, winter and summer? How can we deny that there is an invisible Presence, Life, and Power acting intelligently as the visible universe? How is it possible not to accept an invisible, all-knowing God capable of operating invisibly in us and through us to bring forth fruitage, harmony, and peace?

Having this higher concept of God as Spirit, All-knowing, All-loving, All-presence, All-power, why can we not rest, relax, live our life and just *be*, knowing that whatever is necessary each hour will come forth in its season? But even though we know these truths, we forget to bring them to conscious remembrance each day. One of the barriers to our progress is that we let truth lie dormant in the back of our mind instead of praying without ceasing.

* * * * *

CONSCIOUSNESS DETERMINES OUR LIFE-EXPERIENCE

Nothing can come into our experience except through our consciousness, so what our life will be depends on what we entertain in consciousness. If we entertain the idea of God as omnipresent Intelligence, Love, and Power, good is going to be our experience.

Our responsibility is to be still and let Omnipresence flow. We need not take thought or plan anything; we just live whatever flows through, which will be every quality of God. Why? Because that is what we are entertaining in consciousness: God. We do not have to think thoughts of generosity, forgiveness, or abundance. We have only to abide in Omnipresence, Omniscience, and Omnipotence, and when we do that we lose all capacity for anything but God, and God flows through. We find ourselves being loving, generous, kind, and pure, but we have not had to take thought about it.

What is in a consciousness that is not imbued with Omnipresence? What is left when God is taken out of our consciousness? Fear, ignorance, superstition, desire, anxiety, concern, get, give me, help me, I, me, mine! When God is absent from consciousness, we are living a life with all the accidental happenings that make up the human experience. Only when consciousness is filled with the presence of God is it true that nothing can enter "that defileth . . . or maketh a lie."[2]

Holding good thoughts will not be a protection to us. The only protection is holding thought on God. There is no use thinking thoughts of safety or security or thoughts of abundance. Such thoughts will never bring these to us. A consciousness imbued with God is a consciousness full of love, life, forgiveness, sharing, peace on earth.

We cannot have a consciousness filled with God and fail to understand that all mankind is really God in manifestation. Mankind as a whole is not showing this forth because it is ignorant of its true identity, just as we were before we were awakened. If our consciousness is filled with God, nobody has to tell us how to act, because there is no way for us to act: there is only a way for God to act in us and through us.

CONSCIOUSNESS EXTERNALIZES AS FORM

As soon as even a small measure of spiritual illumination is attained and that Consciousness which is God becomes realized as our individual consciousness, It becomes the substance of all form and the harmony of life. Consciousness appears outwardly as form.

At one time a practitioner-friend who needed to make a trip to Europe left his entire practice in my care. When he came back, he said his patients were so pleased with my work that he felt he should go to another part of the city and set up a whole new practice. I explained to him that he could not do that even if he wanted to. These patients were his own consciousness appearing as form, and he could not any more give those patients away than he could give away his own consciousness. He could not transfer his consciousness to me, and neither could he transfer his patients. During a temporary absence, he could ask me to care for them and ask them to let me care for them, but that is quite different from giving them up.

Once this is perceived we are forever lifted above any sense of competition at any level, whether in business, art, science, or in the healing or spiritual teaching ministry. Why? Because we do not have customers; we do not have patients; we do not have students: we have our consciousness, and our consciousness externalizes as whatever form is necessary to us. No one can take what is ours away from us.

Once we understand that there is not God *and*, we will know that there is not Consciousness *and*. Therefore, there is not our consciousness *and* our business. Our business is our consciousness in a specific form. When we realize that the customers that we have built into our business with integrity represent our consciousness in form, no one can ever take them from us unless we lose our integrity. The bread that we have cast upon the waters is ours, and it cannot fall into anyone else's hands. It must return to us because there really is no going and no coming. There is no separation between our consciousness and the bread and the water: it is all consciousness appearing.

As we realize this, we will never seek for bread, wine, water, life eternal, companionship, customers, patients, or students, but we will realize that our consciousness appears as these. Then we will see that no sense of separation can ever get in. The only reason you and I do not experience all that the Father has is that there is a *sense* of separation which comes from the materialistic concept that there is a God somewhere: a God and a man, a God that is pure and a man who is a sinner. How are we going to get them together?

I suppose the first thing to do is to persuade the sinning man to be good. But what constitutes being good? If we are Hebrews, it is going to temple on Saturday; if we are Christians, it is going to church on Sunday. Which of these is good, Saturday or Sunday?

How are we going to conform to some kind of good in order to deserve God? The answer is that there is no way to become good enough to deserve God.

There is a way to realize God as our being and discover that because God is pure, our being is pure and then all the impurities are washed away. Whatever is of a negative nature in our experience disappears. It does not happen because we are good, but because God is good, infinite, and omnipresent; and there is no room left for anything but good.

God is infinite consciousness, and therefore, our consciousness appears as form infinitely: our business is infinite; our profession is infinite; and if we are in the healing work, our practice is infinite. If we are spiritual teachers, our student body is infinite. There is no limitation whatsoever unless we ourselves accept limitation.

When Consciousness gives us a work to do, It gives us that work not in order that we may be fulfilled, but that It may be fulfilled. It does not give it to us to do as a sacrifice on our part or to make things easy for someone else at our expense. Always the reason is fulfillment, and what we do as the instrument of that divine Consciousness automatically fulfills us. Everyone who is functioning on the spiritual level of life is fulfilling an inner urge, fulfilling some mission that has been given to him, and his life is fulfilled even if to the world it appears to be a sacrifice.

Those who are on the spiritual path are not on it for glory or for profit: they are on it because there is an urge from God within, a drive that will not give them rest. In spiritual work, I have never yet met a person who had the feeling that he was sacrificing anything.

Rather does he have the feeling that he is being fulfilled, and the benefit to the world is incidental, for he is doing the work for the fulfillment of his own soul and inner life.

When a person does that, he is not sacrificing. It makes no difference then whether or not he is working twenty hours a day and giving away every dollar he earns. It is still no sacrifice because it is done only as fulfillment, or one might say under orders. The higher form of demonstration is to forget the world and think only of attaining one's own highest consciousness. Then let follow what will. Let no one think that he has anything to give the world spiritually until he has attained the conscious realization of God. When he has that, he is given his particular mission to perform.

GOING FROM THE MULISH STATE OF CONSCIOUSNESS TO A RELIANCE ON THE INVISIBLE

To live the mystical life is to acknowledge that everything in the visible realm comes forth from the Invisible. Living the mystical life really means admitting the Invisible into our conscious experience that It may work through us and make visible the so-called tangible universe. This is not by virtue of ourselves, but by virtue of the Spirit which is flowing in us and through us and is evident to those with whom we come in contact. Even beyond this, the influence of our consciousness reaches around the globe. If there is anyone, any condition, or any circumstance a thousand miles away from us of which we have no knowledge, as we open our consciousness and go about our business, in due time that which is ours reaches us no matter from what distance it must come.

"My sheep hear my voice."[3] Everyone who has been imbued with the Spirit has drawn unto himself from throughout the world all that is necessary to his experience. No one of himself can do it. But Spirit, once It is permitted to come into our consciousness, operates in our visible experience and draws to us all that is ours, not only persons, but circumstances, conditions, books, messages, whatever is needed. If the need is for a teacher, It will draw a teacher to us from this world or the worlds that have been or the worlds that are to come. Nothing is impossible to God.

Stillness and listening are our access to Infinity. Every time we believe that we need something or someone, we should immediately go within and realize, "No, no! I have meat the world knows not of. I have the life more abundant."

If we admit having a need, we externalize the need. Whatever the need, it will stay eighteen inches in front of us as long as the word *need* is there, just as in the old Middle West, mules that refused to work or to walk had a bag of food suspended about eighteen inches ahead of them which they could never reach. Every time we say, "I need," we are like those mules, and what we need we have put eighteen inches in front of us. Fulfillment comes only when we accept the truth that we have "meat."

If we find an absence of health, strength, or youth in our body, a lack of what we mistakenly think of as supply in our pocketbook, or a lack of companionship in our life, let us stop being mulish, go back to our Christliness, and realize that even though these are invisible at the moment, the principle of the Master is not "I need," but "I have meat to eat the ye know not of."[4] "I am the bread of life."[5] The Master did not use the future tense. In fact, all spiritual truth is written in the present tense: I have; I am; God is.

THE CONSCIOUSNESS OF NOW

Those who advance far on the spiritual path do so only because, by some miracle of Grace, they have learned to live in the present. They have let the past go by. True, they may refer to it once in a while as an experience, but they do not allow it to influence or affect the present in any way. No matter how distressing the past may have been, how disgraceful or how difficult, a person who permits that to influence today is foolish. The past is gone: it is dead.

There are some persons who have lived eighty or ninety years who let the length of their years on earth spoil their todays by dwelling on how many years of the past there have been and counting how few there are left in the future; whereas there would be more in the future if they would live in the present. Now we are one with the Father. Now. What has that to do with the yesterdays in which we did not know that? Our concern is with the truth we know now, the truth that all that the Father has is ours, and we are going to live in that consciousness.

But what about tomorrow? In the first place, we have not reached that yet, and in the second place, we do not know where we will be tomorrow, or if. Our concern is now, right now. The only thing we have to do with tomorrow is to know that there are things that will come up to be done tomorrow, and we will do them tomorrow. We will not try to do them yesterday or today.

Sufficient unto tomorrow is what has to be done tomorrow.

As we advance on the spiritual path, we will discover that the past fades out, except as a conversation piece, but it has no bearing on our present life, no presence or power. We do not give it jurisdiction; we do not allow the fact that we do not have as much education as somebody else has carry any weight, nor the fact that somebody else has more money than we have affect us. Nothing concerning the past has to do with us.

I live in the now. Now I open the door of my consciousness. Now I admit the Christ, the presence of God into my consciousness, and I let that work in me as I go about my daily tasks.

We must live in and as God-consciousness, never limiting ourselves. While we may not show forth all of Infinity on earth, we probably will show forth a greater measure of Infinity than we ever dreamed that a human being could show forth. All of it breaks through with the words *as* and *is*. There is no God *and*; there is only God; but God functions *as* the life of individual being. God functions *as* the mind of individual being, *as* the intelligence and wisdom. God functions *as* the substance and the law as we abide in and live with that *as* and *is*.

Since God is infinite and constitutes our being, our very being contains within itself everything that we shall ever need from now unto eternity. All we have to do is to stop trying to acquire or attain, and to let that which is already embodied within us appear outwardly as form.

Our consciousness contains all that we need tomorrow, next week, next year, and unto eternity. To bring this into activity, we must develop the practice of meditation in which we can be beholders and watch as these things appear in our life. It makes no difference what we wish to draw from within ourselves, it is already there. But we must develop that inner beholding which creates a vacuum. Then, whatever we need flows into expression, whether it is business, employees, more capital in our business, or a new idea for advertising. It does not exist in time and space. It exists within our consciousness, and we must develop a mode of prayer which becomes a listening attitude so God's grace can flow out from us. It will, if we live and move and have our being in the realization that God is our consciousness, and consciousness is the substance of all form and activity necessary for our life.

It is this primal, first Consciousness, first Cause, God, our individual consciousness, which appears as whatever form is necessary to us, and no one can take it away from us because the form is in our consciousness. No one can take our money away from us because our supply is not money: our money is our consciousness of supply externalized. Those who lose it lose it for only one reason: they have not learned that money is not something separate and apart from God. If God is infinite, money must be a part of Infinity; and if God is our consciousness, then our money is part of our consciousness, as are our home, our family, and all that pertains to us. No one can take them from us. Neither time nor space can take them from us for they exist not as material form, separate and apart from consciousness, but as Consciousness Itself appearing as individual forms.

~9~

THE ISSUES OF LIFE ARE IN CONSCIOUSNESS

Spiritual consciousness is the opposite of all we have been taught from infancy. For one thing it is a reversal of the commonly accepted idea of substance as that which we can see, feel, touch, or handle.

So much effort is put into acquiring money, property, or merchandise that the world places its value in these things. Why are wars fought? Why are political elections held? Why the eternal struggle to try to own a business or create a monopoly? Is it not primarily for the purpose of acquiring money, property, or merchandise? All the thousands of years that this has been going on, people have not learned that even after these things are acquired there is no assurance of their being able to hold onto them or that they will buy the things they hoped to get.

A gross materialist does not work for money for the sake of getting money. He believes that the money will buy something called satisfaction, pleasure, security, peace of mind, or power. Few persons think that money in and of itself is valuable. Even the man who owns a gold mine is not satisfied to keep the gold. He has to translate it into some other substance. Everyone who struggles for money expects to trade it, or some of it, for those things called peace of mind, health, or power.

It is the same with those who gormandize. It is not the food they care about. Always in connection with the eating or overindulgence in food or drink is the belief that the indulgence will bring satisfaction.

Where the materialist differs from those of spiritual vision is that the materialist believes that he must first accumulate the matter and then exchange it for spiritual values. In that he fails. The person of spiritual vision does not believe that spiritual qualities can be purchased with money, property, or merchandise. Rather he has arrived at the realization that they come from some fountain within his own being having nothing to do with money, and that a person may have no money and have more peace of mind, satisfaction, and joy than the person who has more than enough money for all his needs and desires.

Those of us who have gone through life seeking satisfaction in the outer realm already know how unsatisfactory the process is, and to what degree we fail. Seeking our good in the outer world has not produced what we have sought. That is why we are on the Path.

In our evolution from material sense to spiritual consciousness, we learn that there is an invisible substance called God, Spirit, Soul, or Consciousness. The name is not important. The important thing is that there is an invisible substance within our own being, and out of it the good things of life are formed. "Faith is the substance of things hoped for,"[1] which we interpret to mean that Consciousness is the substance of things hoped for, and out of Consciousness come the issues of life.

TRANSFER POWER FROM EFFECT TO CAUSE

We are up against generations of world belief that the organs and functions of the body can be and do something of themselves and that they can determine the issues of life, that they can act in such a manner as to cause disease and ultimately death, as if they contained the intelligence to govern our existence. In truth, the dominion was given to us in the beginning.

No organ or function of the body in and of itself has the intelligence to be healthy or to be sick, to be active, overactive, or underactive. No part of the body can determine for itself what it will do or how it will act or when or why. The consciousness that formed the body in the beginning is the Consciousness that maintains and sustains it.

Since it is our state of consciousness that has accepted the belief that the organs and functions can act of themselves, it must be our consciousness that rejects that belief and accepts the truth that God gave us dominion through Consciousness, and that this Consciousness is the cause and the creative principle of our body.

THE NUTRITIVE VALUE OF FOOD IS IN CONSCIOUSNESS

One of the major things that seems to throw our bodies off balance is food and the claim that it has power over us. I am sure you have all seen food frying, boiling, or broiling in the pan. Is it not foolish to look at it and think that it has power over us? Actually it hasn't. That the nutritive value of food is in the food is a belief that has been handed down to us through generations.

The truth is that the nutritive value of our food is in our consciousness. It is not in the food at all. We first have to impart to that food its value before it can nourish us. We have to give it its power to harm us before it can harm us. All of us have done that from childhood by saying, "This doesn't agree with me, so I won't eat it, and if I do eat it, it will upset me. If I drink coffee at night, it will keep me awake."

The world belief is that certain foods provide necessary elements and substances for the body, and according to material standards of life, no doubt that is true. When nutritionists tell us that vitamin A does one thing and vitamin B another let us not doubt but that they do. And when they tell us that we require so many calories a day, it is probably true. It would be foolish for anyone to deny that in the human picture vitamins and minerals are effective. But if they were doing their work and if the organs of the body were functioning perfectly, many of us probably would not be looking for something that would give us a greater sense of well-being.

Human belief, universally accepted, claims that life is in the heart, the liver, the kidneys, and in the digestive and eliminative organs. We have become victims of that belief. The truth is that in and of themselves the organs of the body cannot move and cannot operate. If we believe that the digestive organs can digest separate and apart from consciousness, we have failed to see that the body of itself is just a piece of dead flesh. There is an *I* that governs and controls the body and the entire situation.

The unfoldment that came to me, however, is that the food we eat does not nourish us. It is the Soul at the center of our being that imparts to the food the value that we are to derive from it. In reality, all food that we take in is harmless, and if it has any qualities of world belief that are harmful, it cannot hurt us since our enlightened consciousness does not empower it to be harmful, and in and of itself it is not harmful. As many times as we eat each day, let us realize that whatever of value there is in the food comes from our consciousness. This we must do with food. Sooner or later we must do it with the organs and functions of the body. As we come to a measure of spiritual consciousness, we learn the great lesson that nothing in this world of effect has power.

All power is in God at the center of my being, and God at the center of my being imparts to my bones, to my flesh, and to my food all the energy and power that they finally have in and on me.

The Consciousness that formed me is the government of my body. The Consciousness that created me maintains and sustains every action, every organ, and every function of my being, and that same Consciousness imparts to the food I eat its qualities of good to me. It is the very substance of the food I take in, and that Consciousness determines its health-giving and nourishing value to me. The food itself does not determine its qualities of nourishment, nor do the organs and functions of the body. The Consciousness that formed the food and that formed the organs determines the harmony and activity of my body and the value of the food I eat.

I consciously withdraw power from the outer realm and place it where it belongs: in Consciousness. Here and now I agree that Consciousness governs every function, organ, and activity of my body, and I no longer accept the belief that weather, climate, food, or anything else is a governing factor in my experience.

If we accept and believe this truth, food, as such, cannot be the determining factor in our experience. Food of itself has no power; food of itself cannot possess any maintaining, sustaining, or nourishing qualities, since the same Consciousness that governs and controls the organs and functions of the body must govern the quality of the food we eat. We consciously realize the divine government of the body, not merely to have a better digestive or eliminative system, not merely to give us a better figure if we are too thin, or to reduce our weight if we are too heavy, but once we catch this principle as applied to food, organs, and functions, we will have caught the entire spiritual principle of life. Every issue of life is determined, not by external conditions and things, but by Consciousness.

Within us are the issues of life, not in somebody or something. If we can prove this principle in one instance, never again will we have a false desire or an unsatisfying desire. Every desire will be normal, natural, right, harmonious, joyous, and abundant, and it will fulfill itself. To prove in one area of experience that the Infinite Invisible is the real substance, law, and activity of our existence is to find ourselves quickly independent of person, place, or thing. We will have made our contact with God, and from then on, God will supply everything necessary for our unfoldment and spiritual welfare.

At least two or three times every day, we should realize that Soul, the intelligence and the life of us at the center of our being, is governing and controlling our body. The body is not controlling us. We control the body. There is a Soul at the center of our being, and it must be a daily realization that Its function is to govern and animate our body intelligently and harmoniously, not only today but eternally—not just threescore years and ten, but on to 120, 130, or 140 here on this plane if we choose. There is no limit to the length of time that the body will function except the limit of universal belief that we accept.

It takes discipline to become accustomed to the idea that neither the body nor the actions and functions of the body determine our health, but rather that health is determined by Consciousness, and that Consciousness animates, governs, and controls the organs and functions of the body.

SPIRITUAL SELECTIVITY

We should eat intelligently, eat what we know is good for us at our stage of consciousness. That does not mean making a fetish of it. The person who is sensible about his eating habits realizes that it is not what goes into the mouth, but what proceeds out of the mouth that is important. It is what comes out of one's consciousness that feeds the body, maintains, and sustains it. We must act intelligently in our dietary habits, eating the things we like while avoiding the more destructive kinds of food according to universal belief and then giving it no further thought. If we live each day in meditation and contemplation of the word of God, we will be fed from within. "I have meat to eat that ye know not of."[2] That meat is the inner meat, the inner bread.

Many people believe that bread is the staff of life only because of what Scripture says, but that was never meant in a literal sense. It means that the word of God is the staff of life, and abiding in it, food will never bother us to too great an extent. There will not be an overindulgence, nor will there be an under indulgence. Our elevated state of consciousness will prove to be selective, so that gradually we will discard food that for us is not particularly acceptable to our system.

That does not mean that food is either good or bad, but it does mean that there are states of consciousness which will not take too readily to some foods and will take to others. Not knowing that, we have formed the habit of eating almost everything we like. But spiritual selectivity will sometimes tell us not to eat meat for a week or for two or three weeks or to drink a quart of water daily. That is not a reliance on matter: that is a spiritual selectivity, bringing to us our need in a language intelligible to us at a given moment and at a given state of consciousness.

In our modern way of living, everything that is put in front of us is not really food, even though it is dressed up as food on the table. When we go to restaurants, we eat what is set before us. It cannot harm us because it is not a power, but neither would we want to spend our whole life eating what from a human standpoint is not food. So in our homes we should have the intelligence to use bread, pies, or cakes that are baked of flour and other substances that have real food value.

If at this level of consciousness, we find that we are not getting enough of certain vitamins in our food, what difference would it make if we should take them in the form of a capsule or a pill? It is the same as food. As long as we tabernacle in the fleshly sense of body, we have to eat, and the food we eat will carry with it some measure of world belief, and the measure of that belief

will determine our comfort. As we work with the
principle of one Substance and one Power, world belief
will have less and less power in our experience and we
will be living out from our God-given dominion.

POWER IS IN CONSCIOUSNESS

We must pass from the belief that something external
has power over us to the realization that all power is
derived from God and is given to us. Whether it is the
organs and functions of the body, the food we eat, or
the climate or weather outside, it is our consciousness
that determines its good in our experience. When we
realize this we have made a transition out of material
sense into spiritual consciousness.

Now we no longer look outside for our good but to
Consciousness, and It appears outwardly as food,
transportation, or home. We do not become ascetic and
deny whatever of good comes, but enjoy it, knowing
that it has come from the divine Consciousness within
us.

So, also, we do not look to friends for companionship.
We realize that the Soul-power at the center of our being
appears outwardly as friends. Humanly, those who are
friends today can be enemies tomorrow. That could not
be true if we realize that only the God-power at the center
of our being gives them the power of friendship with us,
because there is one Soul, functioning as each one of us.

The essence of the mystical life was revealed by the
Master when he said, "I have meat to eat that ye know
not of." When Jesus was hungry and the temptation
came to him to turn stones into bread, he said, "No,
none of that for me. I'm not interested in food on the

outside. 'Get thee behind me, Satan.'[3] I'm not making any miracles around here." He knew that at the center of his being was the God-power that would feed and sustain him, and when It was ready to bring bread to him, the bread would be there. God at the center of his being would produce it.

There was no call for Jesus to jump off a cliff to prove that his life was eternal and that God would sustain him. God was sustaining him on top of the cliff. Why jump off? He was being sustained and was satisfied where he was. That was all that was necessary. He did not have to prove it. It was going on. Life is going on for us, and as we realize that this Life which is our life is Self-sustained and Self-maintained, we will make less effort to improve it, and then we will find it taking care of itself.

God, the Self-Created and Self-Maintaining Principle

It is reported that a professor who was working on a project in connection with hydrogen was addressing a group of scientists and physicists on some new phase of the experiment. He began by saying that he knew that there were some of those present who still believed in God. "I must tell you that to understand this experiment and the higher experiments in nuclear fission, you must accept the fact that there is no God. And not only must you accept it, but you must believe it. I am not telling you this from a religious standpoint: I am speaking from the standpoint of what I have proved in the laboratory. There is no God, and you can drop all that nonsense right here and now. I have proved that everything that exists in this world is hydrogen in some form, shape, or manner. There is nothing existent that is not composed of hydrogen."

One of the scientists looked up and said to him, "But, Professor, where does the hydrogen come from?"

"Oh," he replied, "that is self-created and self-sustained."

And this man commented, "I thought that was God."

At that, the professor stood stock-still and said, "You are right. Whatever name you give it, it is self-maintained, self-sustained, and self-created; it is the Infinite." And he himself was convinced.

If that professor could have understood that there is a self-created and a self-maintained Substance, he would have understood also that the substance of all form is eternal, immortal, and governed by that same self-creating, self-created, and self-maintaining Principle or Substance. Surely we must be able to go as far as this learned man and agree with that. We must recognize that the organs and functions of the body, the food we eat, the air we breathe, or the rain or snow that falls is of that self-created and self-maintained Substance and Activity which the professor called hydrogen, but which we call God. Because of that, there is no evil in any of those things.

This brings us to the highest law of mysticism: in reality there is only one Power in this universe, all good, and there is nothing evil. We can make anything evil in our experience by thinking it so, but that does not mean that it is of itself evil. On the contrary, if we can posit a principle of a self-created and a self-maintaining infinite Substance, then we must logically go the next step and recognize It as the only Substance. If It is Self-created and Self-maintained, It must be good or It could not last eternally and immortally; and if It is good, It is good in any form in which It appears.

Everything that exists was formed of the one basic Substance we call God, Soul, Spirit, Life, Principle, or Law. That Substance is within us, and our realization of this makes It the law to the organs and functions of our body. It becomes the law even unto the food we eat, and it is that Substance at the center of us which is the only nourishment that food can have.

Every time we eat a morsel of food, usually we take in, not only the food, but the world belief about the food: some of it is fattening and some of it is thinning; some of it is good for us and some of it is bad for us. Since no change takes place in our life except through the activity of our consciousness, it becomes necessary for us to realize every time we eat:

The substance and the activity of me are derived from God at the center of my being, and I can respond to no other thought or thing. I impart the activity, the nourishment, the satisfaction, the taste, and the pleasure to this food. I, Consciousness, Soul, Spirit, at the center of my being, give unto the organs and functions of my body their capacity to digest, assimilate and eliminate, or whatever else the body has to do.

SURMOUNTING WORLD BELIEFS THROUGH AN ACTIVITY OF CONSCIOUSNESS

Through an activity of consciousness, we transfer all power from the outer world and place it where it really belongs: within us. Dominion has been given to us by God over everything that exists, but we must consciously exercise that dominion. Consciously, we have to come back to the center of our being and for weeks and months realize that dominion until it becomes automatic. The first few months of this study are very difficult. It takes discipline to remember where power is, how power is derived, and what real substance is.

Every time we are tempted to think in terms of money, consciously we have to reinterpret this and realize, "No, the power, substance, and supply are within me, not in dollar bills—within me. If they were in dollar bills, a dollar bill would always buy the same thing. It does not. The power of supply is within me, within my consciousness, which determines my supply."

No one can avoid the responsibility for spiritual realization and for developing a consciousness of one Power. We pay the penalty for whatever belief we accept, until that belief is corrected. Whatever of good comes into our experience comes through the activity of our consciousness in accepting the truth and rejecting universal belief by consciously remembering every day:

God at the center of my being is the law of my experience, and It is the law of love unto me. God at the center of my being is the substance and the nourishment of the food I eat. God at the center of my being is the law and the activity unto every organ and function of my body. God at the center of my being is the law and the activity of the weather and the climate.

God at the center of my being draws unto me everything necessary for my good. It acts as a law of elimination to everything not necessary to my spiritual unfoldment and development.

It is something to remember three times a day that all power is at the center of our being, vested in our

Soul, and that our Soul is the substance, the law, the activity, and the reality of all that concerns us. Only in proportion as we know the truth can it make us free. Substituting truth for universal belief is an activity of our consciousness, and that makes it operative in our experience.

We live as human beings under the laws of belief, including every law that *materia medica* has set down, even those that ten years from now we will not accept as laws at all. These laws are operative in our experience just as Santa Claus operates as a law unto a child until he learns that Santa Claus is a fictitious character, and after that Santa Claus becomes nothing more than a name to him.

So it is that these laws of *materia medica*, of food, and of climate are really Santa Claus experiences in our life. They are nonexistent powers, but they operate as real until we consciously eliminate the belief and exchange it for truth. That, no one can do for us except temporarily. That is why we can have healings from practitioners, but we cannot have our life made over. Only we ourselves can make our life over, and the way is to give up these universal beliefs as fast as we discover that they are beliefs and come to the realization that *I*, God, at the center of our being, is the substance and Soul of our being, and It is governing our whole experience.

That divine Consciousness to which we open ourselves in receptivity takes over and fulfills our life. But we have to let It in by opening our consciousness to that *I* within us which is All-wisdom. If it is possible to let that *I* which is God take over, It lives our life and fulfills our experience. It has a better will for us and more power to fulfill Itself and Its good than we have, and It does it in a much better way than we can ever plan it.

A good illustration is the experience I had when I first went to Portland, Oregon, to speak. If I had tried to tell God what I wanted, I never would have thought of the most important thing that came to me on that trip because I knew nothing about it. Fortunately, my prayer then was as it is now, "Father, fulfill Thyself."

So when I came to the Center and was asked if I would object to having the talk tape recorded, I had not even heard of a tape recorder and knew nothing of its function. Since that time all my class and lecture work has been tape recorded, and through that instrument it has been made available to students for all time. I was not praying for something, but just leaving myself open, and what came, came by the grace of God.

For this effective way of spreading the message of The Infinite Way, I could not have prayed, nor could I have asked God for it because it was as totally unknown to me as atomic power was unknown to us a few years ago. It walked in by Grace, and is now serving an important purpose. A new way of teaching and presenting truth had opened up. Through what? Through the ability to be receptive so that when a new idea was presented, there was a willingness to accept it. A door was opened because my prayer was to open consciousness to whatever form of good God sends even if it is one about which I know nothing.

We may think that we know what would be good for us tomorrow or for the balance of this year, but I can assure you that God has good for us that we could not dream of and would not ask for. Personally, I do not care what happens tomorrow. The way is so completely open with me that whatever God determines, that is the

way it will be, and I am not going to be egotistical
.enough to try to tell God where I think I should be or
what I think God should have me do tomorrow or the
next day or next month or next year. We do not go to
God to have certain things brought about for tomorrow.
We go to God with this attitude:

*Today, tomorrow, and all time to come, God, I belong to
You. Map out my days.*

As we sit quietly and peacefully, listening intently, it
will not be long until Something says to us, "Go to bed;
it is all right;" or "Go on now and do your housework;"
or "Go to business. *I* am on the field." It does not have
to say it in those words, but there will be a feeling of
rightness. There will be a release of the burden, a
dropping away of fear. Something will come bringing us
a sense of assurance that God is on the field.

This is the transition from material sense to spiritual
sense. Every day we whittle away some world belief and
substitute an activity of truth, until we reach the ultimate of spiritual living where we do not have to take
thought. Something at the center is always doing things
for us: bringing the right food to us and rejecting the
wrong; bringing us the right friendships and taking from
us those that have no part in our experience; bringing
the right opportunities to us and seeing that we do not
take advantage of the wrong ones.

Always there is Something at the center of our being
so that we find ourselves saying, "Heavens! I'm not
living my own life any more." That's right. We are not.
It has taken over and It lives our life for us. So we can

say, "I'm not digesting my food." And we are not. It is digesting it. We have no conscious thought in the matter. We do not have to take conscious thought for any phase of our life: we let It take over and live it. Then we understand that the divine Consciousness within us lives our life, and we just watch what It does.

~ 10 ~

THE CONSCIOUSNESS OF TRUTH
IS THE HEALER

If all the people on earth could be brought to a spiritual experience, they probably would not care too much if they were healthy or sick, wealthy or poor. The Experience itself is enough without these added human things. The healing ministry is important, however, because when a person has experienced a spiritual healing it sets up a longing to go further than just being healed. It brings out in him a desire to know God, to live the spiritual life, and then in turn to be able to help others.

There never has been and never will be a teaching that will enable anyone to heal. The letter of truth alone will never heal or reform anybody, but the letter of truth will provide a person with principles which, as they are incorporated into his consciousness, enable him to release himself from material sense and evolve into spiritual consciousness. It is spiritual consciousness that heals, the spiritual consciousness with which some few mystics have come into the world. Spiritual healing is accomplished through either the natural or developed spiritual consciousness of a person, and that spiritual consciousness is yours and mine when we no longer

117

turn to God for healing or believe that there is a God withholding healing, a God who will do today what He was not doing yesterday.

The degree of help you will be able to give anyone is dependent upon the truth that is embodied in your contemplative meditation or treatment which becomes realized consciousness, the very substance and essence of the healing. A person who has been active in the healing ministry for several years should be doing effective healing work. By the time he has worked with these principles day after day, and night after night, his whole consciousness becomes so imbued with truth that there is little of humanhood left.

The practitioner who has worked with enough different types of cases comes to realize that the words he has used in his meditations or treatments in the first year are really true. When he was using them then, he did not really believe them. He was merely declaring some words that he hoped were true. But after working with truth for several years, there is no longer any need to declare or voice it because as soon as a patient flashes his troubles across the mind of the practitioner, the practitioner immediately recognizes them as mirage, illusion, *maya*, or a claim of two powers, and they are thereby dissolved.

There is no mental effort in spiritual healing; there is no mental effort on the part of the practitioner: there is no effort at all. The effort comes in developing consciousness to the point where there is the actual experience that God is life and that your patient has no life other than God, no other mind, no other Soul, no other being. Then must come the realization that the appearance which the patient has brought to the practitioner is but a shadow, an image in mind.

The moment a claim is presented to you, recognize it not as a person, but as a mesmeric picture of a selfhood, a law, and a life apart from God, as having its cause in the universal belief in two powers, a belief so universal and mesmeric that to some extent everyone is a victim of it.

In these first years, you must work definitely, specifically, and often with the principles. Be willing to work with them religiously until you prove their truth and that practicing them does result in fruitage. As you continue practicing and working faithfully with the principles two, three, or four years, you will be declaring them less and less. The day will come when, regardless of the name or nature of the claim that is presented to you, you will automatically realize its impersonal nature and non-power and turn away from it. You may do this 80 or 90 percent of the time, but 10 or 20 percent of the time it may be necessary to go deeper.

All Claims Are of a Universal Nature, but Some Persons Personalize Them

All persons are not equally receptive. In some cases, healings will not come until a change of consciousness is brought about in the patient. You are not a healer of the body; you cannot remove disease. It is a change in consciousness which produces the outer effect of healing. Usually, however, most healings can be complete and quick because the claim the patient is suffering from is of such a universal nature that it has nothing to do with him personally except that momentarily he is the victim of it. As soon as the universal belief is dissolved, he is free.

Occasionally, a patient clings to some belief which at the moment he is not able to surrender. It has become personalized with him, and in that case your work may have to continue until there is a release from that. For example, the fear of death is a universal belief, but it becomes personalized with some persons when they reach the fifties and sixties, and consciously or unconsciously, their thinking changes because they have accepted the belief of ultimate death. Sometimes your treatment may have to continue until they awaken to realize that they are immortal whether here or there. Then they are released.

With others it may be something of a personal nature. But be sure that you do not fasten it onto them. Even if it is uncovered to you, do not tell the patient that he must get rid of it. Whatever is uncovered to you, let it drop as a nothingness, remembering that neither you nor the patient has anything to get rid of. What you have to do is to know the truth, and the constant knowing of that truth will build a whole new consciousness in which error, regardless of its name or nature, will have less and less power until finally it has none.

CONTEMPLATIVE MEDITATION OR TREATMENT LIFTS CONSCIOUSNESS

Some of the problems that may present themselves to you continue to maintain the appearance of reality in spite of your recognition of their unreality. In such cases, you may have to work with these principles until you are elevated so high in consciousness that the Spirit of God takes over. Your treatment consists first of consciously realizing within yourself the nature of God: the allness, the omnipresence, and the omniaction of God.

God is the lawgiver, and because of the infinity of God, all law is spiritual law. There is no other. Then what about this material or mental law? In the allness of spiritual law, material or mental laws must be lumped together as part and parcel of the carnal mind or nothingness and, therefore, inoperative. Through such treatment, infection and contagion are nullified without their even having been mentioned. It nullifies hereditary laws, laws of food, climate, weather, and the law of threescore years and ten, which is one of the most diabolical laws operating in human consciousness.

When a person recognizes God as infinite, omnipresent Life and then realizes that all the evil that comes to his eyes and ears is only the projection of the belief in two powers and is not a person or a condition, his fears drop away. He becomes quiet inside, and in that stillness something takes place which cannot be described. He cannot see what it is, hear, taste, touch, or smell it. He merely knows that he is in a state of calm. That calm is the presence of the transcendental Something that dissolves the erroneous pictures. It does not heal disease: there is none. It does not reform sinners: there are none. It dissolves the belief in good and evil, and when that is dissolved the person is no longer seeing "through a glass, darkly."[1] He is seeing face to face.

God governs, maintains, and sustains Its own creation. God is my life, my mind, my soul, and my being, and the only law operating in, through, and as my consciousness.

I need not fear what mortal man or carnal mind can do to me. I need not fear what infection or heredity can do. I need not fear any material or mental powers for the omnipresence of God is my robe. Into this, nothing can enter to destroy or disturb: no universal belief, no activity of the carnal mind, nothing of any nature that the world calls destructive. The omnipresence of God reveals the nothingness of the carnal mind, of all its activities and whatever its so-called history.

The carnal mind does not operate as a person or thing: it operates only as a belief in two powers. I do not accept that belief because I accept God as the one Power.

Did God make the carnal mind? No, the carnal mind and all its activities are nothing. They are this universal human mind arising out of the belief of good and evil, a belief which has no real existence. In reality, there is no mind to be called "carnal."

Did God create any law, any being, any power, or anything anywhere any time that could destroy Its creation? No, the infinity of God eliminates all possibility of God ever having created anything destructive to Itself, and there is no other creator or creative principle.

A patient receives the benefit from the practitioner's help because he has made contact with the practitioner, and the truth the practitioner knows in his consciousness becomes the law unto the patient. It is never the truth when there is a "you" in the treatment because the "you" who is being addressed has just told the practitioner that he is sick. How, then, can he be the child of God? How can he be spiritual or perfect or immortal? A human being is never immortal or spiritual. He cannot be. This work is undertaken to make the human being "die daily,"[2] so that he may be reborn of the Spirit. Is it not foolish to tell that human sense of self which is to "die" that it is already spiritual?

Do not give anyone a treatment or take a person into your meditation. Forget those who have turned to you for help; turn to the Presence within. By remembering and rehearsing these specific principles you bring yourself to the place where you no longer fear the appearances that are brought to you. You cannot hate error anymore, nor can you fear it, because now you have witnessed that, in and of itself, it is not a power; it is merely a belief.

The purpose of your treatment or contemplative meditation is to assure and reassure yourself as to the truth of these principles until you are so elevated in consciousness that you can settle down with "Father, it's Your turn." Then you wait, sometimes seconds, sometimes minutes, until you feel a response, a release, or you may even receive a message. Then you know that God is on the field. It is not your treatment that brings God onto the field, but your treatment elevates you in consciousness to where you can be receptive to the presence of God, which was already there, but which you could not receive through the human mind.

Do not believe that your prayers or your treatments have any effect upon God. It is *you* that they affect. In proportion as you work with specific principles which impersonalize the error and nothingize it, you are relieved of your fear. When you no longer fear "man, whose breath is in his nostrils,"[3] or the condition of that man, it is because you have attained communion with God and have received within yourself God's assurance that these things are not power: Fear not, they have only the "arm of flesh."[4] You have the Lord God Almighty–all might, the only might. If God has all might, "the armies of the aliens"[5] have no might. If God is all might, sin, disease, and death are not might.

This is not using truth to overcome anything. This is using truth to bring you to the realization that there is no other power to be feared. You need abide only in Immanuel, God with you, in the realization that all evil has its source in a universal belief, and, being impersonal, it has no person in whom, on whom, or through whom to operate.

As you work with these principles, you are developing a measure of the healing Christ-consciousness in which, when the appearance touches you, you need not reach out to God for anything for you already have the awareness that God is. You will be elevated into a state of consciousness where you become receptive to the Presence within. "Where the Spirit of the Lord is, there is liberty,"[6] and that liberty is for all those who bring themselves to your consciousness.

When you no longer seek a God-power for anything, when you have attained the state of consciousness revealed in the Twenty-third Psalm and are convinced that the Lord is your shepherd, you have gone beyond the metaphysical into the mystical state of consciousness.

THE PRACTICE OF SPECIFIC PRINCIPLES DEVELOPS CONSCIOUSNESS

The object of Infinite Way work is to bring your consciousness to that place where you rise above merely a belief in God and come into the experience of communion with God. Then you no longer have any beliefs about God: you have the Experience.

Just as Joseph, after being thrown into a ditch and sold into slavery, reached Egypt where his destiny was to be fulfilled, so many of us, either through sin, disease, lack, or threatened death, have been pushed into a metaphysical or spiritual teaching and in that way to the realization of God. From then on, there is no limit to our measure of realization except such limit as we place upon ourselves by inertia or by an unwillingness to dig in and work until we attain this consciousness.

You cannot come to the spiritual throne until you love God supremely, and you are loving God supremely only if you acknowledge God as the only Power. Only in Omnipresence can you lose your fear of "man, whose breath is in his nostrils." Because of Omnipresence, God constitutes individual being, and you recognize mortality as nothing but an illusion of sense. You do not try to heal it, cure it, or get rid of it: you recognize it as the nothingness it is.

If you can be made to fear, be assured you will be somebody's slave sooner or later. You cannot be free while you fear germs or bombs, persons or conditions. You can never be free until you come to the realization that you are one with the Father. Eventually you learn to walk up and down this world singing within yourself:

I and the Father are one, and all that the Father has is mine. Right inside of me is the bread, the meat, the wine, and the water. Right within me is the resurrection, life eternal. Wherever I go, I carry it with me. "If I ascend up into heaven, thou art there: if I make my bed in hell, behold, thou art there."[7] If "I walk through the valley of the shadow of death,"[8] what is within me goes with me. An invisible Presence goes before me to "make the crooked places straight" [9] and prepare "mansions" [10] for me.

I do not have to speak of this outwardly or openly. Knowing this truth inwardly, secretly, and sacredly, the invisible "Father which seeth in secret" [11] goes before me to reveal fulfillment on the outer plane.

You develop this consciousness by the practice of specific principles and by working with them, whether you take them in through the spoken or the written word. You will not make spiritual progress merely by reading books and hearing truth. It is what you do with truth after it has touched your consciousness that determines the degree of your realization. You must take these truths and live with them, ponder, meditate upon them, and keep them ever alive in your consciousness, until one day they will fall from the head into the heart. After that, they are always present as a realized state of consciousness.

Once you have reached the place where you no longer hate, fear, or love the so-called evil powers of the world and are able to respond without fear to epidemics, storms, depressions, or diseases of one nature or another and can prove by your state of consciousness that these are not power, never were and never can be power, that they exist only as temporal power when you give power to them, you will have touched the Source of life, the divine Consciousness which is yours.

* * * * *

THE IMPERSONAL NATURE OF ERROR

In your contemplative meditation realize that God is the substance of all being and the law of all being. God constitutes all being, and God is performing His function in you without your reminding, bribing, or asking Him. You need not pray to God for health; you need not ask God for healing. God already knows your needs, and it is His good pleasure to give you the kingdom. God is already in the midst of you, so rest in the understanding that God is and that God is functioning.

After your meditation on the allness of God is completed, you may still be faced with whatever the seeming problem is. So you come to the most important principle of healing work. Error is not personal; therefore, it has nothing to do with you, with your patient, or with your student. Furthermore, in trying to bring through a healing you need not try to improve your patient, correct him, analyze him, or try to make him a better human being. If he could be a better human being, he would be it without your help.

Drop the patient, the disease, or the sin from your thought, while you realize that this problem that is confronting you is an effect. Remember that: it is an effect. An effect of what? Wrong thinking? No. An effect of sin? No. An effect of heredity? No. An effect of something in the body? No. It is an effect of the carnal mind, the belief in two powers.

When you are confronted with a problem and have awakened to the point of realization, you can say, "Oh, carnal mind," and turn over and go to sleep, because you have recognized it as the "arm of flesh," or nothingness. You have not said, "Carnal mind! Now, how shall I destroy it?" or "Oh, disease is an illusion. How shall I get rid of the illusion?" You have done what you would do in the desert after you have realized that the water that you are seeing up ahead is a mirage. You do not turn around and say, "Well, now, I must get a pail and get rid of the mirage." No, while it was water, you may have thought of getting a pail, but once you have perceived that it is a mirage, you start your car and go forward because you are not afraid of a mirage.

In your healing practice, you will never be afraid of any case, no matter how long it may have lasted, once you have stopped the habit of dealing with it as if it were a disease, and wondering if you have enough understanding with which to meet it.

One of the first principles that revealed itself to me in the form of an inner illumination was that you cannot meet a problem on the level of the problem.* If you try to treat a cold as a cold, it will get the best of you. Do not believe that a cold is a cold: a cold is a belief in two powers, a belief that there is God and another power. When you are confronted with a fever, do not try to reduce it. Do not ask the patient an hour later, "has your temperature gone down?" A fever is not a fever; it is a temptation to believe in two powers. It is a temptation to believe that God is not the substance of all form, that God is not Omnipotence, and that there is some Power you have to call up to do something.

In every case that comes to you for healing, your first step is the realization of God as constituting all being. Work with that idea until you have an inner assurance

---

*The Infinite Way, by the author.

that God is. Then impersonalize the evil–the error or the appearance–whatever its name or nature, by consciously knowing that it is no part of a person and that all evil is impersonal. It must be seen that evil is not in, of, or through person; it is not appearing as person; it is something separate and apart from person. It is impersonal evil, and because of the nature of God as Omnipotence, it must be nothingness. Sin, disease, and death have nothing to do with God. God did not create them, and if God did not create them, they can have no existence apart from the mind that is believing in two powers.

Every student must work with these principles until he develops Christ-consciousness. This does not mean that a student should not ask for help when he needs help. It does not mean that he must arbitrarily and with willpower determine that he will meet a particular problem himself. There is not much virtue in that. It does mean that, as problems come up, the student works with these principles and tries to meet the problem himself, but if he does not quickly meet it, he should turn to someone else for help.

In the beginning your treatment may last fifteen or twenty minutes. Later on your treatment may take only three or four minutes, and the time will come when thirty seconds will be much more time than you will need for an average treatment. A treatment does not take place in time or space. It is an activity of realized Christ-consciousness, your individual consciousness when it no longer fears anything or anybody in the external world.

~ 11 ~

THE FOURTH-DIMENSIONAL CONSCIOUSNESS

Working and living with a message such as The Infinite Way and being on a path of this nature, there comes a time when a transition is made from living a normal human life in which we make decisions and accept responsibilities to one in which we become aware that we are not alone, but that there is Something else. Whatever it may be or however the experience comes to us, we have a feeling that Somebody or Something is very close to us, governing our life.

We find ourselves going in directions that we had not thought about or planned, and perhaps doing a work that we had never before dreamed of. There is always an awareness of the Presence going before us to "make the crooked places straight,"[1] walking beside us as protection or behind us as a rear guard. Whether we feel It as a Presence or as Something very personal will probably vary with each one of us. To me, It is always a Presence or a Spirit, and not often but sometimes when It speaks to me, It is an audible voice. Most of the time, however, It is just an awareness.

After enough years had gone by in my life, it was certainly clear to me that I was not a writer, and yet a book came forth, out of which the whole activity of The

Infinite Way was born. So it must be evident that there is Something that gave me this message, these principles, and that brought forth publishers and money enough to carry The Infinite Way around the world. That Something is behind the message of The Infinite Way, and I am merely the instrument through which It is functioning.

Eventually, Spirit makes Itself evident to all those who work faithfully with these spiritual principles. It does not duplicate through them the work of The Infinite Way because that would not be intelligent. But It has been responsible for the editing of these writings and for raising up teachers, who have felt the Spirit to the extent that they also are but instruments through which the Spirit is projecting The Infinite Way into human consciousness.

It is Spirit, also, which is responsible for whatever healing work is accomplished, because the letter of truth alone will not do it. There must be this accompanying Spirit, otherwise some of us would claim to know how healing is brought about. As far as I am concerned, it is not possible to know that because when healing takes place something happens within that brings an assurance to the person giving the help that all is well.

So it is that in meditating with students, not only individually, but when we are together in classes or lectures, the object is to bring Spirit into realization, that is, to abide in the meditation until the Spirit within announces Itself in some way.

As we watch this work, we can see what happens to a student who is meditating regularly with a spiritual teacher. The first day, the first week, or the first month, he may not notice any change in his life, although he may. On the other hand, he may be aware of very dramatic changes within himself, but not necessarily. As we look back on a group of students after a few years, we begin to see the changes that have taken place in their consciousness, changes that are made manifest in their physical appearance, in their dress, and perhaps in their increased sense of supply or health. This is not the result of treatment or of a specific meditation, but it is the fruitage of continued meditation during which time that Spirit works in them and begins to change their consciousness.

Students often find it difficult to understand why these changes cannot be made more rapidly. By now you must understand that any change that takes place in a person's life, mind, or body takes place because of a change of consciousness within him. It has nothing to do with any miracle-worker or with any kind of abracadabra, such as, "You were sick, but now you are well;" or "You were poor, but now you are rich." It is nothing of this nature. When a person who has been touched by Spirit and has consciously realized the indwelling Presence touches another person's consciousness, something takes place within that person. He responds, even though he knows nothing about how it occurred. At the moment, it may have brought forth no visible or tangible response in him whatsoever, or he may have felt something and then later forgotten about it. But one thing is certain: from that first contact, when Spirit touched his consciousness, It is working in him, and from that time on, It brings about changes in him.

These changes may be rapid or they may be slow, depending upon the resistance that is within the student. The resistance within any one of us is not something for which we are responsible. It is nothing that we can change by wanting to be rid of it right away. The resistance that is in us is the cumulative effect, not only of all that we have experienced in this life, but perhaps many of the things that we brought with us of which we are not even aware. Whatever it is, the fact remains that there is within every one of us a resistance to Spirit, which if we want to be honest, we may call the Antichrist. It is something in us that will not permit us to respond to the spiritual influence. Consciously or unconsciously, we are holding onto something.

THE MATERIALISM OF HUMAN CONSCIOUSNESS MUST BE SURMOUNTED

One of the major barriers to attaining spiritual realization is the materialism that exists in our consciousness for which none of us is responsible. In our early experience, almost every thought we had about God also brought forth some thought of what material good would follow. We have thought of God, Spirit, in terms of Its bringing forth more bodily health, material wealth, or more harmony. This is natural. Let no one deny it and let no one be ashamed of it. We were born into a materialistic consciousness where, to us, good means more health, more wealth, more happiness, or more peace, all on the human plane.

No one had taught us that there is a place called "My kingdom,"[2] and nobody had ever told us that there is something called "My peace"[3]; and that this "My kingdom" or "My peace" has nothing to do with "this world."[2] It is another realm. But in the early stages of this transitional experience, our interest is not in the other realm: our interest is in whether or not some lump can be removed, our income doubled, or whether we can have more happiness at home. The barrier is that when we come to the spiritual path, we are not thinking in terms of the Christ-kingdom or that peace the world cannot give.

As we come under the guidance of a spiritual teacher and a spiritual teaching, and as we practice meditation, Spirit begins to work in us. Our consciousness changes, and we think more and more of the spiritual mystery and miracle: spiritual consciousness. We have what metaphysically is called demonstrations on the human level, but now instead of merely rejoicing that the pain we had is gone or that we have a little more income, our attention is being turned from the effect to the Cause. Now we are gradually attaining enough spiritual wisdom so that as our human picture unfolds beautifully and harmoniously, we are grateful and are beginning to understand that there is an invisible Something producing the visible effect.

As more and more we go behind the human scene and recognize that whatever of good is taking place in the visible world is the result of our awareness of the invisible Presence, a great transition begins to take place in our consciousness. We even have momentary feelings of that Presence, little touches of Grace, and we become more and more aware that operating invisibly is Something of which we humanly are not aware.

In Christian mysticism, this Presence is known as the Christ, but the term that describes It best is *transcendental.* There is a Something that transcends our ability to describe, to know, or even to contemplate. It is Something outside the range of human thought, and yet we know It is there because occasionally we have glimpses of It or see fruitage from It.

Every harmonious effect that takes place in our life after we have begun to meditate is the direct result of the transcendental Presence, even though at first, we may have no awareness of the Invisible. We are aware only that we had a pain and that it is gone or that our human life is changing in some way for the better, or our consciousness, nature, and our habits are changing. It may be that we are finding more pleasure in, and using more hours for spiritual study, reflection, or meditation.

All this eventually reveals to us that what is happening in the tangible world is the fruitage of what is happening in the invisible world. It is all taking place because within us is the spiritual seed, which has always been there, not only since we were born, but since the beginning of time when we first appeared, coexistent with God. In the beginning, there was God and God's creation. There cannot be God separate from creation, nor can there be a creation appearing some time later than God. God and God's manifestation of Himself are always simultaneous.

There is a transcendental Presence, the Christ, within every person, but the person who is not aware of It is that "natural man"[4] who is not under the law of God. This same person aware of the indwelling Presence becomes the child of God. The Spirit of God, which is always present, becomes tangible to him at a particular time as he becomes aware of that which always has been there with him.

* * * * *

THE FOURTH-DIMENSIONAL CONSCIOUSNESS BRINGS SPIRITUAL DISCERNMENT AND TRANSCENDS TIME AND SPACE

When we are human beings who have not yet realized the Presence, we are living in the three-dimensional consciousness, a three-dimensional mind, and insofar as we are concerned, the only reality of life there is, is what we know through the physical senses.

The Master through his fourth-dimensional Consciousness not only had access to a place he called "My kingdom," the invisible realm behind this visible one, but through the fourth-dimensional Consciousness, he could, when necessary, read the minds of those about him. It was not by any human means that he perceived the nature of the life that the woman at the well was living, but through living in the Fourth Dimension, he could see into the third dimension and discern her state of consciousness. In this way he was able to select his disciples, the best that were available at the time, those most able to stand with him, those most able to grasp what he had to teach, and those most nearly ready for the Experience.

As our spiritual vision increases and our spiritual consciousness unfolds, we, too, will have the gift of discernment in some degree and be able to see some of the experiences of the past, the present, and the future. At first, we will probably wonder what is happening to us, but all that is happening is that we are now manifesting some measure of the fourth-dimensional Consciousness which enables us to see into the human mind.

This sometimes happens with practitioners when, in working with a patient, they are able to discern the particular error that is binding him and then nullify it. It

is only because they have risen into some measure of
the Fourth Dimension that they can see into the third
dimension, see what is wrong, and correct it.

It is sometimes called intuition, but it goes far beyond that. When we receive direct instructions as to
what to do when we ourselves had planned on something entirely different, or when things arise that must
be done and the human situations which would interfere
with and interrupt them are suddenly removed, then we
realize that Something cleared the way for us.

I believe that if one rises high enough in consciousness, it is possible to look back into previous lives. It
may be that these glimpses of previous lives are given to
those who have some reason for knowing about them.
We can understand how a man like the Master may
have been puzzled about why he was having the experiences he was having. Here he was in an unfriendly
world with a strange message which was bringing forth
a different response in different places. In his moments
of mountaintop experiences, however, parts of his past
may have been revealed to him to show him why he
was on the Path, what the meaning of his ministry was,
what his part in it was to be, and what his previous
preparation for it had been.

Many mystics have not only had knowledge of their
past experience, but they have also had knowledge of
previous contacts with some of their disciples or followers on the Path. This was the experience of
Ramakrishna when, for the first time, he met
Vivekananda. Vivekananda had not even wanted to
meet Ramakrishna and had canceled all appointments
he had made to hear him. Then one day when he could
no longer refuse, he went to meet the man, and at first

sight they knew each other. It is reported that at that first meeting Ramakrishna said to Vivekananda, "Why have you taken so long? I have been waiting for you for centuries."

Vivekananda became Ramakrishna's number one disciple, gave up everything in life, went to live in the ashram with Ramakrishna, and then went out into the world to carry on perhaps one of the greatest missionary works in modern days. I know of no other person who has traveled throughout the world as did Vivekananda presenting his teacher's message in a far better way than his teacher could have presented it and in such a way that made it acceptable and led to its establishment in many places.

So it has been with other spiritual teachers: they have recognized someone whom they had known before, or a student has recognized a teacher whom he had known before. When a person is lifted into the higher consciousness, he can look back into the lower one, just as a college student can look back into high school books that once might not have been understandable to him but are now clear. So does the fourth-dimensional Consciousness see into the third-dimensional, perceive the things there, and benefit by what is seen.

THE TEACHER-STUDENT RELATIONSHIP

The relationship between teacher and student is an eternal relationship, if the student will have it so. This is true of my relationship with those students who have been drawn to me. Never, never will I be separated from my serious students, not by time or space, nor will I be separated from them by life or death because I know that all that constitutes me in reality is Consciousness. Therefore, I can hold in my consciousness "my own," those with whom I desire to companion. Nothing will ever separate me from the love of my serious students or from sharing with them.

Throughout my lifetime, I have found that my greatest joy and my greatest fruitage have been from companionship with my serious students, those who love The Infinite Way, those who benefit from it, and those who rejoice in their study of it. These students have been my companions for many, many years. They have really constituted my spiritual household. For this reason, I have lived in consciousness with my students very often early in the morning, and very often late at night, and very often in between. Where our treasure is, that is where we are going to be, and mine has been with spiritual seekers.

Since consciousness is what I am, I embody in my consciousness all that belongs to me. And since in the kingdom of God there is no such thing as time or space, this all happens now and this all happens here where I am. You may look outside and see a sign which says *Hawaii,* and that is where I am and that is where it is happening. But if you look outside and see a sign which says *California* or *London,* that is where I am, and that is where it is happening. Why? Because it is happening in Consciousness, not in a city or state or a country. In Consciousness we are never separated. We are all one in our spiritual identity and in our spiritual household.

Open your consciousness and realize that I do not exist in time or space. The only place I can exist for you is in your consciousness. If you let me out of your consciousness, you have let go of me because all you can know of me is what you can embody in your consciousness, and this is not dependent on physical sense.

So in praying for a person it is not necessary that the person prayed for and the person doing the praying be in the same place. What is necessary is the realization that we exist *as* and *in* and *of* Consciousness, and in Consciousness we are one. We are not physical beings: we are offspring of God. That which constitutes the physical frame is only of relative importance. It is here today and sometimes gone tomorrow. There is no such thing as an eternal physical frame. Why? Because I am not a physical frame, nor are you.

No Separation in Consciousness

Many people ask questions such as: "Will I be reunited with my family when I pass on?" or "Will my family be reunited with me in the next world?" My answer has always been: "It all depends on you, and it all depends on them. If you want to be reunited with them, you will be. If they want to be reunited with you, they will be. But if you do not wish to be reunited, you will not be because you exist as consciousness and you can admit into your consciousness or drop from your consciousness whomever you wish."

Certainly, this is true even here on earth. Are we in touch with all our relatives? No, we have no interest in some of them, and they have no interest in us, so we drop out of each other's consciousness. But there are loved ones from whom some circumstance of life or death has separated us. I can tell you that no one who enters my life or my consciousness will ever be separated or apart from it—in life or in death—except those with whom I have nothing in common and whom I am willing to have dropped from me. By the same token, they are more than glad to drop me from their consciousness.

Have we ever received any benefit from another except the benefit of consciousness? Is it not a person's consciousness that blesses us? What part of me has ever blessed any student except my consciousness of Truth? What part of him have I known except his consciousness, his love for Truth, his love for Spirit? We are one in Consciousness, and one we will ever be as long as our interest is in Truth, Spirit, God, Consciousness. Thus, in the absence of our loved ones, for any reason, there will be no sense of loss or sense of separation because we will know that we have no physical relationship. Our relationship is one of consciousness.

Each one of us however, must be prepared for the day when our loved ones will leave us in what the world calls death. But this is not really separation because what we love of each other is not the body: it is the consciousness. If God has breathed into us the life of God, then the life of God is the life of man, and we can never be separated from our Life, not even in death because "I and my Father are one"[5]: I and my life are one, I and my love are one, one and indestructible.

All the misery of humanhood arises from the belief that we are separate one from another, from our friends and relatives, separate from our supply, our home, our employment, and our country. Every discord on earth arises from the sense of separation. The unifying principle is that we are one with the Father, inseparable and indivisible, and in oneness with God, we are one with infinite good, which must include companionship, relationships, supply, home, employment, activity. There never would be a discord on earth if there were not a sense of separation from God, for only in our relationship of oneness with God are we one with one another. If we become one on any other basis, it is not a permanent relationship. Not every family remains together forever, and yet they would, if that togetherness were originally based on the understanding of oneness with God.

"My oneness with God constitutes my oneness with all spiritual being and with every spiritual idea or thing."* No one would ever be separated from supply if his supply were based on his relationship with Deity. When we understand that our oneness with our Source constitutes our oneness with supply, then we know that what God has joined together, no man *can* put asunder. Does man have a power that can separate God from His own? This would be giving to man a power greater than God's.

Our supply is ours only because "I and my Father are one" and, therefore, we are heirs to all the heavenly riches. In our understanding of that, no person or circumstance can separate us from our supply. Our relationship with God builds up whatever in our experience appears to have been lost.

All competition arises from a sense of separation from God and from the belief that I am here, you are there, and there is something out here that we both want. What difference does it make where I seem to be or where you seem to be in time and space, or where our supply seems to be, since nothing has ever escaped out of

---

* *Conscious Union With God,* by the author.

our consciousness because God constitutes our consciousness?

Rising Above Human Consciousness

Every time we are faced with two powers in the world and remind ourselves that there is but one Power, the power of the Spirit within us, we are lifting ourselves higher in consciousness. Every time we remind ourselves that we are not using God to do something to evil but rather that we are recognizing the nothingness of the appearance of evil, we are developing the fourth-dimensional Consciousness. Every time we impersonalize evil and nothingize it, realizing that it is no part of man but is the universal belief in two powers, we are destroying a part of the third-dimensional consciousness and developing that much more of the fourth-dimensional Consciousness.

Every time we consciously impersonalize and realize that neither sin, disease, nor false appetite is a part of our being but that it is merely a universal belief in two powers, that, too, is developing our spiritual or fourth-dimensional Consciousness. Every time we recognize that *I* in the midst of us is God—that this *I*, the individualization of God within us, is really the Source of our supply, health, and harmony—part of the old man is "dying," and part of the new is being reborn, part of mortality is being put off and immortality is being put on.

Every time we meditate, even if it is only a ten-second meditation, just enough time to create that vacuum and to listen, we are developing our consciousness to the fourth degree. An onion skin of mortality is dropping off, and we are that much closer to immortality.

Every effort we make to gain more of the fourth-dimensional Consciousness through reading and hearing the words of a spiritual message is destroying some mortality in us, and at the same time, clothing us with immortality. Every meditation that turns us within to let the hidden splendor flow is lifting consciousness to that fourth-dimensional Consciousness.

We become aware that we have a strength, a power, a dominion, and a joyousness that the world knows not of. It knows not the Source, because these spiritual qualities do not arise from external circumstances. It is not because of something in the outer world: it is because of Something within that we ourselves have no knowledge of beyond the fact that we have reached the place where we know that consciousness is what we are. We become conscious of an indwelling Spirit, a divine Presence living within us, going before us, doing all things for us, and bringing to us everything necessary to our spiritual life.

~ 12 ~

CHRIST AS THE CONSCIOUSNESS
OF MANKIND

What is it that sets spiritual teachers and persons who do healing work apart from the rest of mankind? Is it not that in some way, at some time, and for some reason they were drawn to the study of truth? Then as they began to fill their minds with truth through books, lectures, and classes, eventually something happened within them. They made a transition from "man, whose breath is in his nostrils"[1] to that man who has his being in Christ.

At a particular moment in their experience, these persons attained some measure of the transcendental Christ-consciousness, that which is beyond the human. From then on, error, evil, sin, disease, false appetite, or lack lost its reality to them. As persons came to them with physical, moral, or financial problems, or problems of human relationships, the error or evil disappeared just as darkness leaves a room when the light is turned on. The darkness in the room does not go anywhere because what we call darkness is but an absence of light. In the presence of light, there is no darkness.

As mere human beings, we cannot function as practitioners or spiritual teachers. We may have the will, the desire, and the hope; but will, desire, and hope do not heal, reform, or enrich. To lift a person above his humanhood, one must have the experience of spiritual illumination or of the transcendental Presence. When that comes to a person, he is set apart, and in the measure of his fidelity will he be successful as a spiritual healer or teacher.

Many students have the desire to heal, to teach, and to give to others, but they cannot. To these I say, "Be patient: you will. Wait, however, until the Spirit of the Lord God is upon you and you are ordained to do these things." Students must be content to remain students and not try to be practitioners and teachers until the experience that results in their being set apart takes place within their consciousness.

At one time, when the Spirit of the Lord God was upon a person, it was called the coming of the Christ to earth, that is, the coming of the Christ to human consciousness. Today it is believed that almost anyone can attain some measure of that Christ, or Spirit of God. Had it been said two thousand years ago that someday there would be several thousand persons doing spiritual healing work on earth, such an idea would probably have been ridiculed. People would have said that only those whom God visited could do that. Now we know that God visits anyone who can open his consciousness in receptivity to the Presence within.

This has a meaning far greater than anything heretofore realized, because until recently the coming of the Christ to individual consciousness was thought of as a unique experience limited to one person known as Jesus.

THE COMING OF THE CHRIST UNIVERSALLY

Much has been said about the Second Coming of the Christ. But what is meant by the Second Coming? Will it be the return to earth of a man who lived 2000 years ago or will the Second Coming be when the Christ comes to earth as the Consciousness of all mankind, so that forever after there will not be a man, woman, or child on earth in a human state of consciousness?

This day is nigh unto us, the day when the Christ will not come to you or me to elevate us and set us apart from mankind, but when the Christ will come as the Consciousness of all mankind. Then children will enter from birth into the awareness of their spiritual identity and the spiritual identity of all life: human, animal, vegetable, and mineral.

In our work with such things as weather and epidemics, we have already discovered that the realized consciousness of an individual or of a very small group can become the harmonious experience of an entire community. Few in the community then suffer from destructive conditions because these have been prevented or nullified by the activity of the Christ in one individual or in a few, proving that the realization of the Christ as the Consciousness of mankind begins immediately to dispel the mortal sense of humanity.

Every time a person is healed of any discordant condition by the spiritualized consciousness of one dedicated person, it is proof that the activity of the Christ in that one consciousness can be the law of harmony unto multitudes, even of those who have not yet been awakened to the Christ. Furthermore, the activity of the Christ, functioning as teacher, practitioner, or student, does open and awaken the spiritual center of those who come within range of that person's illumined consciousness.

In the past, religion has always worked with the present generation. Even if it succeeded in taking children and adults and leading them up to the point of spiritual consciousness, it always had to begin all over again with the next generation. It had to go through the same cycle, leading them up to an interest in, and awareness of, the Spirit, only then to see them leave this earth.

As we come into the experience of the Christ as universal Consciousness, children and grandchildren will not be born into the mortality of threescore years and ten, but into the immortality of Christ-consciousness, and we will not have to begin again to educate the next generation into spirituality. That will be the promised day when the Consciousness of God is established on earth as it is in heaven, and children are born into It.

As we stop believing that God reveals Itself only to me or to any "me" who has ever lived, we will understand that God has always been revealing Itself to human consciousness. Usually only an individual here or there has been able to pick up this revelation, understand it, and reveal the whole truth, and then have students, disciples, and others later on personalize and destroy the revelations of that realized consciousness.

Every master has known that God does not come to an individual: God reveals Itself in consciousness. Those persons searching, seeking, and reaching for the truth are the ones who first touch it. But now we enter a new dispensation in which we must realize the nature of God as Omnipresence, Omnipotence, and Omniscience *universally*. Omnipresence with me or with you? Is that not a horrible concept of God? Omnipresence does not mean with me or with you. Omnipresence means everywhere equally present with saint and with sinner, with the religious and the irreligious.

If the Christ should come to the consciousness of a person to the extent that he realized his Christhood, and if that person then believed that this was a quality of his own or perhaps even a quality of his followers, it would be a repetition of the experience of the first coming of the Christ, and this grand truth would be lost. But when he realizes, "Well, why me? What is so special about me?" it becomes easy for him to see that this is the truth about anyone wherever he may be at this moment in consciousness, and that everyone must eventually awaken to this truth. The Christ is not the Christ of one person's being only, but the Christ is individual being, the spiritual nature of all being.

CHRIST-CONSCIOUSNESS, THE FOURTH-DIMENSIONAL CONSCIOUSNESS

When we speak about the Christ as universal Consciousness, we are not speaking of anything particularly Christian, because "before Abraham was,"[2] the Christ, the transcendental or fourth-dimensional Consciousness, was. When It touches us, this higher Consciousness transforms us into the son of God who receives the things of God. By what faculty? By the faculty of the mind? No, the faculty of spiritual discernment that enables us to discern what the mind cannot see, hear, taste, touch, or smell.

Why is it that only certain followers of metaphysical movements during the past century have become good practitioners or teachers? Why have there been so few? Why has not everyone who followed the metaphysical movements done outstanding healing and teaching work? The answer is that it is not possible except in proportion as a person attains that higher Consciousness. We must admit that a great many students of metaphysics have not even tried to attain It. As long as they could demonstrate good health, good supply, or good relationships, they were satisfied for the few to become practitioners or teachers.

That era is rapidly passing from us, and the day is coming when there will be fewer practitioners available, and each student will have to be his own practitioner. The Master never intended that one group should be endowed with that divine Consciousness and the rest of the world should live off the consciousness of that dedicated group. The Master's mission was to reveal the Christ as the Consciousness of every individual, that every individual might find fulfillment in the realized Christ.

It is a present possibility for each of us to attain some measure of realization of the divine Consciousness. We may not all attain the fullness of It because it is an evolutionary process. But those with a dedicated consciousness will attain some measure of It in this particular experience on earth, and probably a greater measure of It as they enter future experiences.

The divine Consciousness which was manifested on earth as the great spiritual leaders of the world is here with us now to lift us to that same Christ-consciousness. Because we have the benefit of that Consciousness that has appeared on earth so often in so many forms, we, too, will be raised up to the realization and demonstration of the fourth-dimensional Consciousness.

EVERY PERSON BRINGS UPON HIMSELF THE PENALTY OF HIS OWN THOUGHTS

Here and now, the Christ is being established as universal Consciousness. For this reason we are witnessing something on earth that has never before existed. Today there is already enough of the Christ established as human consciousness so that not only the doing of evil, but the mere thinking of it brings repercussions on the thinker and the doer. In the three-dimensional life into which we were born, men could do all kinds of evil and experience very little punishment. That is why for so many generations we have had wars, slavery, and man's inhumanity to man.

Less and less of that will be possible from now on. There will be less human consciousness: less cheating, stealing, and robbing men of their birthright, and less sending them into wars. The measure of the Christ that is now functioning in human consciousness is sufficient to wreak immediate vengeance upon those who perpetrate wrong, not that the Christ wreaks vengeance, but that the human being brings upon himself the penalty of his own thoughts, motives, and deeds.

Judas Iscariot committed suicide within a few days after his betrayal of the Master. Why did he do that? What made such an act inevitable? Had he betrayed Pilate, he would not have had to commit suicide. He might even have lived to enjoy his money. But no one can do a wrong unto the Christ without its immediately having repercussions upon him, not because the Christ does anything to him, but because in coming into the presence of the Christ, the evil is destroyed. If a person keeps clinging to the evil, it destroys him. But those who can relinquish the evil are healed.

There are thousands of persons desirous of losing not only their diseases but their sins, their false appetites, their resentment, jealousy, envy, malice, lust, and greed. But there are also those who still believe that they can continue to live by the sword and who are not aware that in this age they are going to hit up against the Christ and eventually die by the sword. They do not realize that the weapons they use against humanity are the very weapons that will cut them down and that not in the far future: in the very near present.

There was a time when man's inhumanity to man could make men rich and powerful. That time has passed. Today there is sufficient of the Christ loosed in human consciousness so that as evil hits up against It, the evil is destroyed, and the person is set free. Only where a person is determined to cling to the evil and benefit by it is he destroyed along with the evil.

When you and I come in sin into the presence of those of spiritual light, we are healed rather than destroyed. That is because we really do not want to cling to the sin in which we may be indulging, and so when we bring ourselves into the presence of the Christ, we lose the sin, and we hear the Master say, "Neither do I condemn thee: go, and sin no more."[3] If there is sin, false appetite, evil, or any wrong within our consciousness, and we are at the point where we would sincerely like to be free of it, let us seek someone who has attained a sufficient measure of spiritual light to lift us into spiritual consciousness, and we can be set free.

SPIRITUAL REALIZATION RAISES UP CONSCIOUSNESS

Every bit of spiritual light which you and I as individuals attain increases the amount of Christ-consciousness that is loosed in the world. "I, if I be lifted up from the earth, will draw all men unto me."[4] If we attain any measure at all of Christ-consciousness, then those who are receptive respond and are lifted into a higher measure of Christ-consciousness and experience physical, mental, moral, or financial healing.

Where there are groups who have studied for years and attained some measure of spiritual light, hundreds are being drawn to the light; and when there are hundreds who have attained spiritual consciousness, then thousands will be drawn to that light. Any measure of spiritual light that is raised up in a person immediately begins to raise up some member of his family, some neighbor, friend, relative, or stranger. This bears witness to the truth that the measure of the Christ raised up in one person is the measure of the Christ loosed in consciousness to raise up others.

As we acknowledge the Christ, we are loosing more of the Christ into human consciousness and sin, disease, and death are thereby lessened. The day of living by the sword is passing. In the recognition of the Christ of our being, the Christ is on earth now instead of mortal man, the Christ as universal identity.

SPIRITUAL PIONEERS

We are witnessing the ushering in of the Second Coming of the Christ, the coming of the Christ to human consciousness universally—not merely to saints and sages, nor to the few who become practitioners. No, the Christ is now coming to earth as the Consciousness of mankind. You and I are ushering in that age in this recognition:

Consciousness is what I am. Christ is my individual consciousness and yours. Everyone who touches me anywhere on life's journey must automatically be lifted up, if only a grain higher, in spiritual consciousness, with a grain less of sin, a grain less of disease, a grain less of old age, a grain less of false appetites.

As we consciously begin to realize the Christ as the identity of every individual, we are establishing the reign of the Christ on earth. We are part of a pioneer movement. We do not have to belong to any teacher, teaching, or religion. Every one of us is the temple of God, and our relationship with God has to do with an activity of our own consciousness in which we realize that we are heirs of God, joint-heirs to all the heavenly riches, to the omnipresence, omnipotence, and omniscience of God.

In acknowledging this and thereby bringing to ourselves the harmonies which automatically follow the reign of the Christ, we are bringing these blessings to the entire world. We cannot wait for three billion people to decide to turn to truth to save the world because nearly all of them will pass on before they attain a consciousness of truth. Then we will have to begin all over again with the next generation of four billion, and they, too, will pass on before their consciousness is transformed.

Let us stop trying to reach mankind and instead raise up the Christ within us and realize that same Christ in everyone, thereby establishing the reign of the Christ on earth. Then the three billion will discover that they are God-governed.

When that day comes, if we witness it, we probably will be surprised that those who have been benefited or blessed by this realization are not grateful for it. They will never be grateful because they will not know out of what they have been lifted. We have evidence of this in our work. It used to puzzle me years ago when I would witness beautiful healings of so-called mental cases. The shocking thing was that those healed never said a word of thanks, nor did they ever express any gratitude. Then I realized that they never knew that they had been mentally disturbed at all. They knew themselves only as they were after being healed. So the new generation that is born into Christhood will never be grateful for it, because it will never know from what it was saved.

Christ-consciousness is now evolving on earth, and as It continues to evolve, the new generation will be born into that Consciousness. What we are developing through study and meditation, it will be born into. The old world will be wiped out and disappear, and a new world will be born.

Every truth realized in consciousness becomes a law unto consciousness. But how can it be confined to a single person? It does not become a law to a person: it becomes a law unto consciousness. The person most nearly attuned receives the first and greatest benefit, but eventually the circle widens, and even friends and relatives who cannot directly accept a spiritual message begin to show forth some measure of good.

Those who are realizing spiritual principles are forming the consciousness of the new generation. This process did not begin with us. We are the recipients of all the spiritual wisdom of Lao Tzu, Gautama, Jesus, John, and Paul, and of all the spiritual wisdom of the mystics of the world, which has helped to form our consciousness. That which was placed in consciousness by the mystics of all time has enabled us to be born, not as savages, but as persons with some degree of civilization. A higher consciousness is evolving in the world, and all mankind is the beneficiary of it.

God's grace does not bring anyone to a message of this nature for his good alone. God's grace does not work that way. God's grace brings us to a spiritual teaching that we may show forth the fruitage of Christ-consciousness and be instruments for establishing It on earth. Every truth that we know and every healing that takes place through our consciousness help to establish that healing Grace in human consciousness.

When we pass from being just human beings into an awareness of our spiritual identity, we become a spiritual influence to hundreds and possibly thousands, ensuring the day of the Christ as the Consciousness of all mankind.

Tape Recordings

The following tape recordings of Joel S. Goldsmith were used in the preparation of this book:

1. The Dedicated Consciousness
   1. *The 1964 San Fernando Valley Center*,
      Reel 1, Sides 1 and 2.

2. The False and Right Sense of *I*
   1. *The 1954 First Portland Practitioners' Class*,
      Reel 1, Side 1.
   2. *The First Northwest Series*,
      "The True and False Sense of *I*"

3. Mind Is a Transparency
   1. *The 1962 London Special Class*,
      Reel 3, Side 1.

4. Consciousness
   1. *The 1963 Princess Kaiulani Sunday Series*,
      Reel 3, Side 1.

5. EVOLVING STATES OF CONSCIOUSNESS

1. *The 1960 Seattle Closed Class,*
   Reel 1, Side 1.
2. *The 1964 Chicago Special Class,*
   Reel 2, Side 1.
3. *The 1963 Princess Kaiulani Sunday Series,*
   Reel 3, Side 1.
4. *The 1960 Canadian Open Class,*
   Reel 2, Side 1.

6. THE LIGHT BREAKING THROUGH

1. *The 1960 Seattle Closed Class,*
   Reel 1, Side 2;
   Reel 2, Sides 1 and 2.
2. *The 1964 Chicago Special Class,*
   Reel 2, Side 1.

7. ATTAINING A MEASURE OF SPIRITUAL Consciousness

1. *The 1962 San Diego Special Class,*
   Reel 1, Side 2.
2. *Spiritual Consciousness*
   (tape not available).
3. *The 1960 Canadian Open Class,*
   Reel 2, Side 1.

8. INVISIBLE LIFE FULFILLS ITSELF TANGIBLY AND
VISIBLY
   1. *The 1960 Seattle Closed Class,*
      Reel 3, Side 1.
   2. *The 1960 Canadian Open Class,*
      Reel 2, Side 1.
   3. *The 1964 Los Angeles Special Class,*
      Reel 1, Side 1.

9. THE ISSUES OF LIFE ARE IN CONSCIOUSNESS
   1. *The 1951 Second Portland Series,*
      Reel 5, Sides 1 and 2.
   2. *The 1959 Special Halekou Work,*
      Reel 3, Side 1.
   3. *The 1954 Seattle Practitioners' Class,*
      Reel 3, Side 2.

10. THE CONSCIOUSNESS OF TRUTH IS THE HEALER
   1. *The 1959 Hawaiian Village Open Class,*
      Reel 4, Side 1.
   2. *The 1959 New York Closed Class,*
      Reel 5, Side 1.
   3. *The 1960 Denver Closed Class,*
      Reel 3, Side 2.

11. THE FOURTH-DIMENSIONAL CONSCIOUSNESS
   1. *The 1962 Manchester Closed Class,*
      Reel 3, Side 1.
   2. *The Honolulu Infinite Way Study Center,*
      September 30, 1963 (unpublished manuscript)

12. CHRIST AS THE CONSCIOUSNESS OF MANKIND
   1. *The 1963 Los Angeles Special Class,*
      Reel 1, Sides 1 and 2.
   2. *The 1963 New York Special Class,*
      Reel 1, Side 1.
   3. *The 1963 London Work,*
      Reel 2, Side 2.

LIST OF SCRIPTURAL REFERENCES

(According to numbered references in text.)

1. THE DEDICATED CONSCIOUSNESS
   1. Isaiah 54:17.   5. I Corinthians 15:31.
   2. Revelation 3:20.   6. Job 23:14.
   3. Matthew 25:40.   7. Psalm 138.8.
   4. Matthew 23:9.

2. THE FALSE AND RIGHT SENSE OF *I*
   1. I Corinthians 15:31.   5. Matthew 20:20-23.
   2. John 5:30.   6. Matthew 19:19.
   3. Matthew 19:16, 17.   7. Exodus 15:2.
   4. Acts 1:24.

3. MIND IS A TRANSPARENCY
   1. I Corinthians 15:31.   5. Isaiah 55:8.
   2. John 4:32.   6. Luke 17:21.
   3. Ecclesiastes 1:2.   7. Galatians 2:20.
   4. Joshua 24:15.

4. CONSCIOUSNESS
   1. John 14.6.   4. Psalm 8:5.
   2. John 10:30.   5. II Corinthians 5:8.
   3. Matthew 18:22.

5. EVOLVING STATES OF CONSCIOUSNESS
   1. I Corinthians 2:14.   5. Zechariah 4:6.
   2. John 15:6.   6. Philippians 2:5.
   3. John 16:33.   7. John 17:5.
   4. Acts 9:5.   8. John 10:30.

6. THE LIGHT BREAKING THROUGH
   1. John 15:16, 19.   3. Genesis 18:32.
   2. Ephesians 4:22.

7. ATTAINING A MEASURE OF SPIRITUAL
   CONSCIOUSNESS
   1. John 16:33   8. I Kings 17:10-16.
   2. John 18:36.   9. Matthew 23:9.
   3. John 14:27.   10. Zechariah 4:6.
   4. Matthew 5:39.   11. John 8:11.
   5. Isaiah 2:22.   12. Matthew 9:5.
   6. Psalm 24:1.   13. John 17:5.
   7. Luke 15:31.

8. INVISIBLE LIFE FULFILLS ITSELF TANGIBLY AND
   VISIBLY
   1. Psalm 42:11.   4. John 4:32.
   2. Revelation 21:27.   5. John 6:35.
   3. John 10:27.

9. THE ISSUES OF LIFE ARE IN CONSCIOUSNESS
   1. Hebrews 11:1.   3. Luke 4:8.
   2. John 4:32.

10.   THE CONSCIOUSNESS OF TRUTH IS THE HEALER
      1. I Corinthians 13:12.   7. Psalm 139:8.
      2. I Corinthians 15:31.   8. Psalm 23:4.
      3. Isaiah 2:22.   9. Isaiah 45:2.
      4. II Chronicles 32:8.   10. John 14:2.
      5. Hebrews 11:34.   11. Matthew 6:6.
      6. II Corinthians 3:17.

11.   THE FOURTH-DIMENSIONAL CONSCIOUSNESS
      1. Isaiah 45:2.   4. I Corinthians 2:14.
      2. John 18:36.   5. John 10:30.
      3. John 14:27.

12.   CHRIST AS THE CONSCIOUSNESS OF MANKIND
      1. Isaiah 2:22.   3. John 8:11.
      2. John 8:58.   4. John 12:32.